Keith Pepperell

Photographs

Keith Pepperell

DEDICATION

To my spawn Jack, Lydia, and Alex all of whom have taken a nice snap of something cool at one time or another

ACKNOWLEDGMENTS

Don Fowler

Audrey Fowler

Pep Pepperell

Joan Pepperell

Who were dab hands with a camera..

THE PHOTOGRAPHS

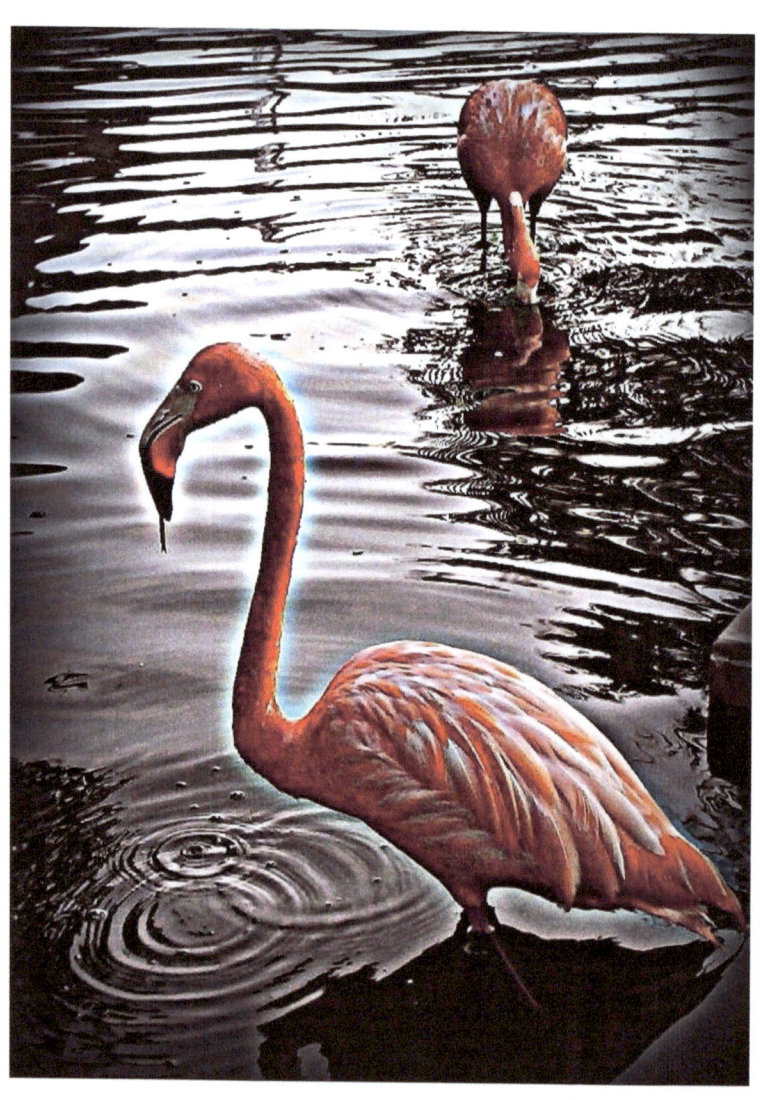

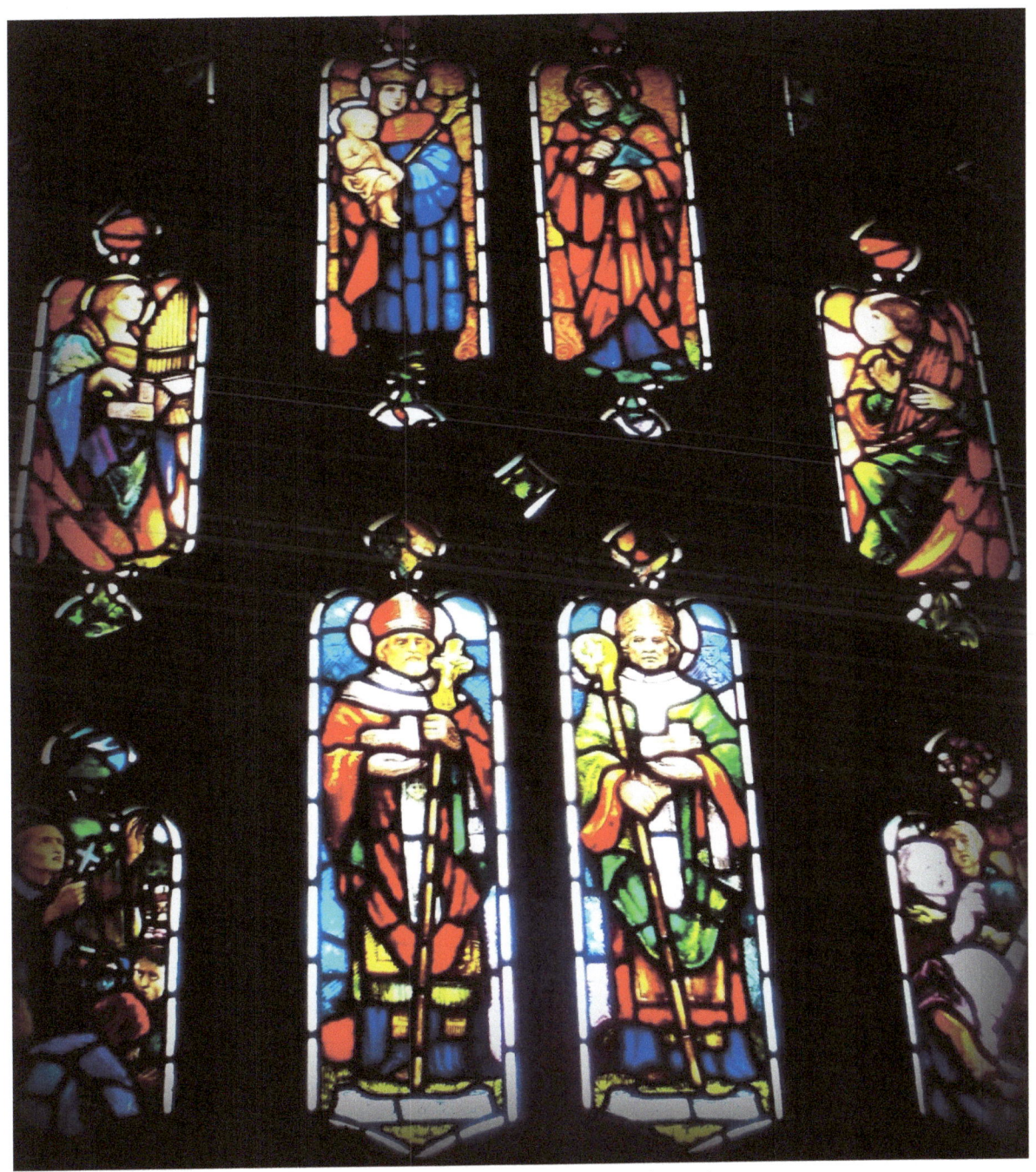

Worcester Cathedral

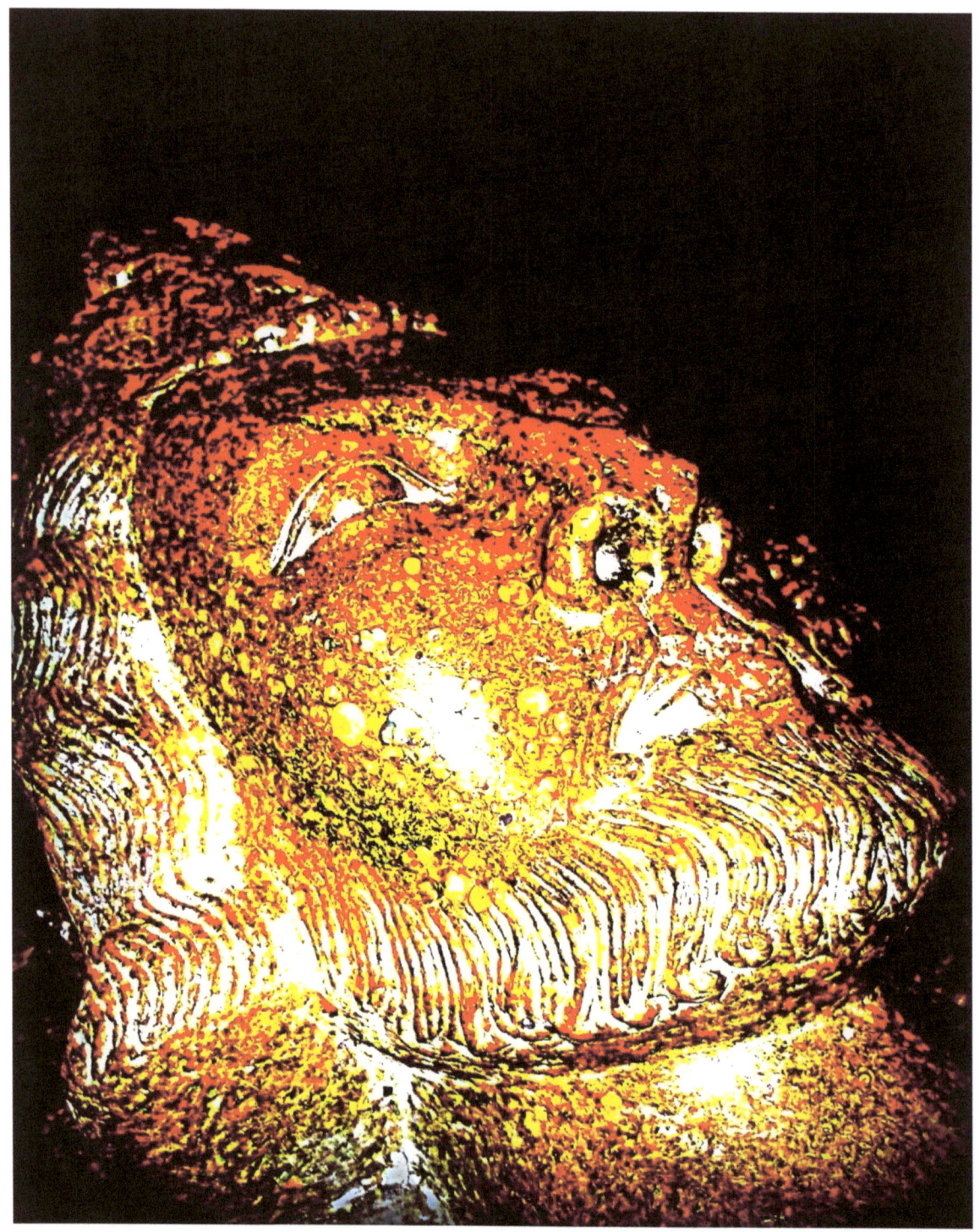

Tomb of King John 1216

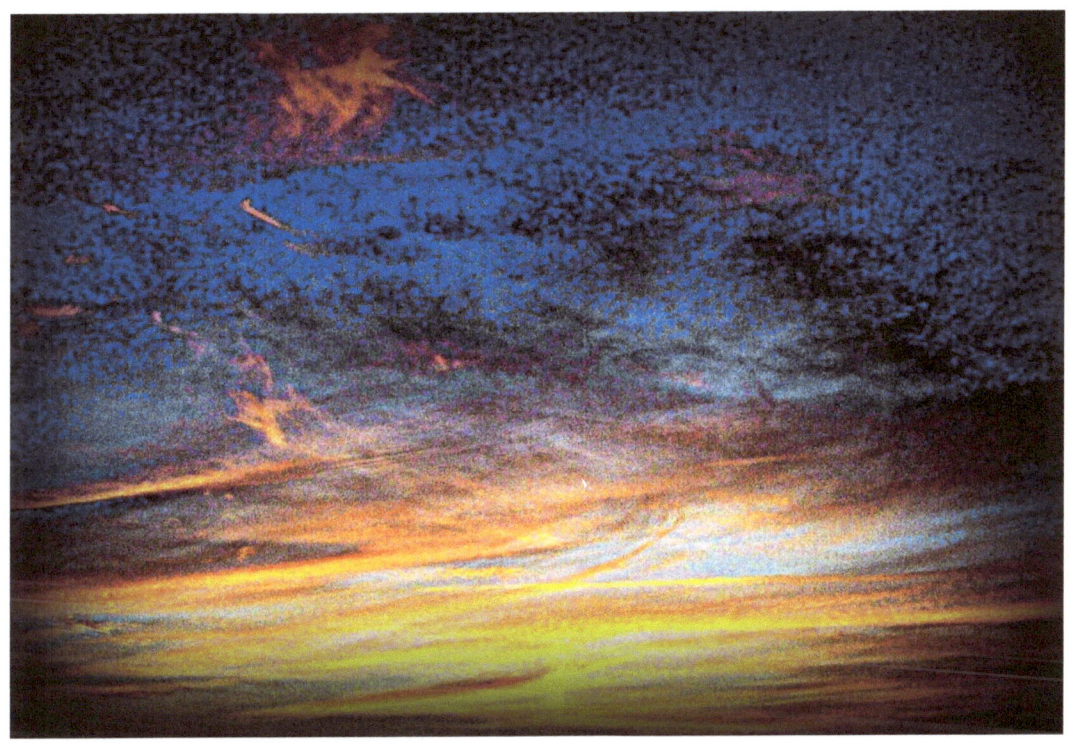

Sunset over Barbados

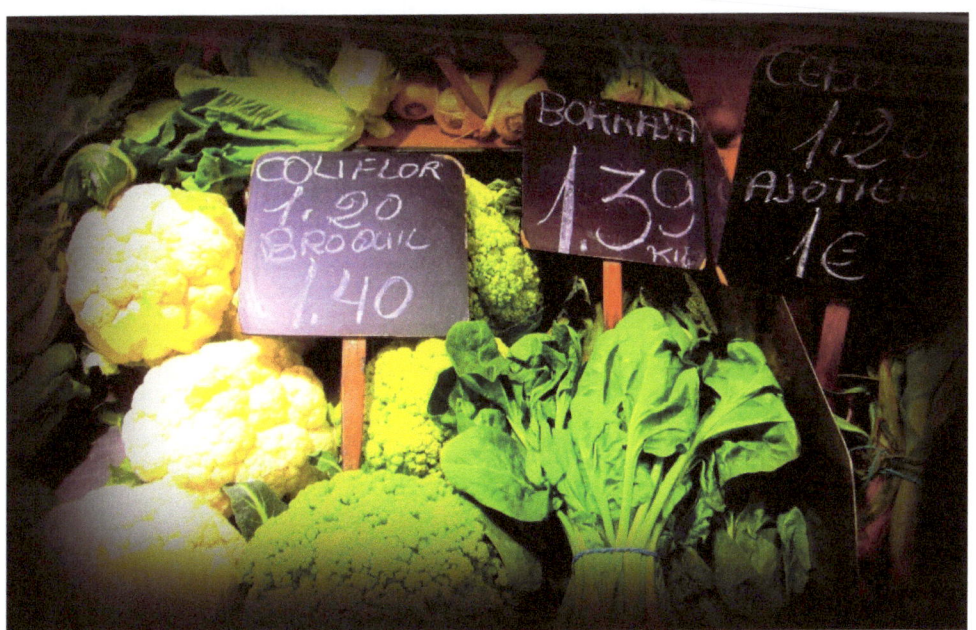

Bahamian Market

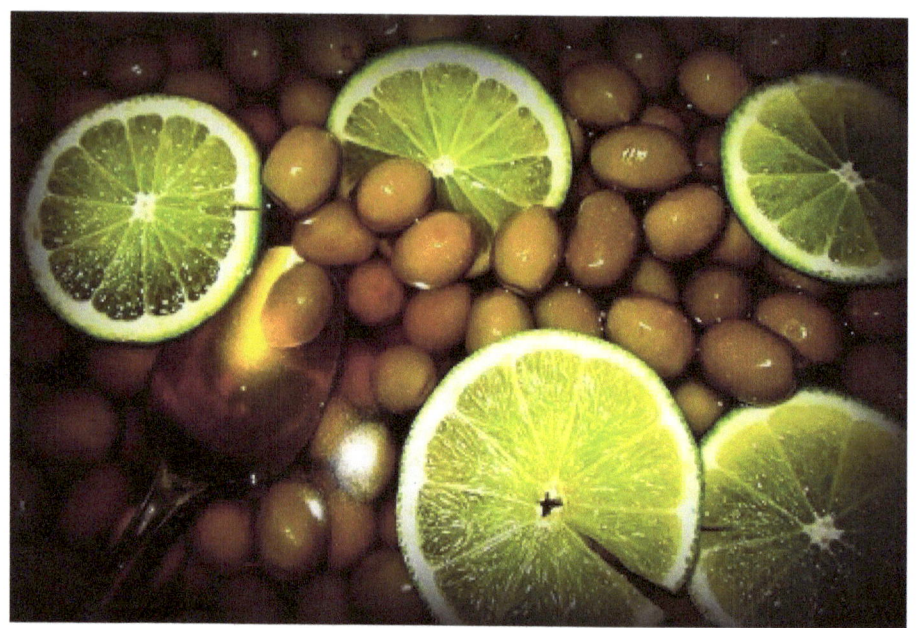

Olives and Limes

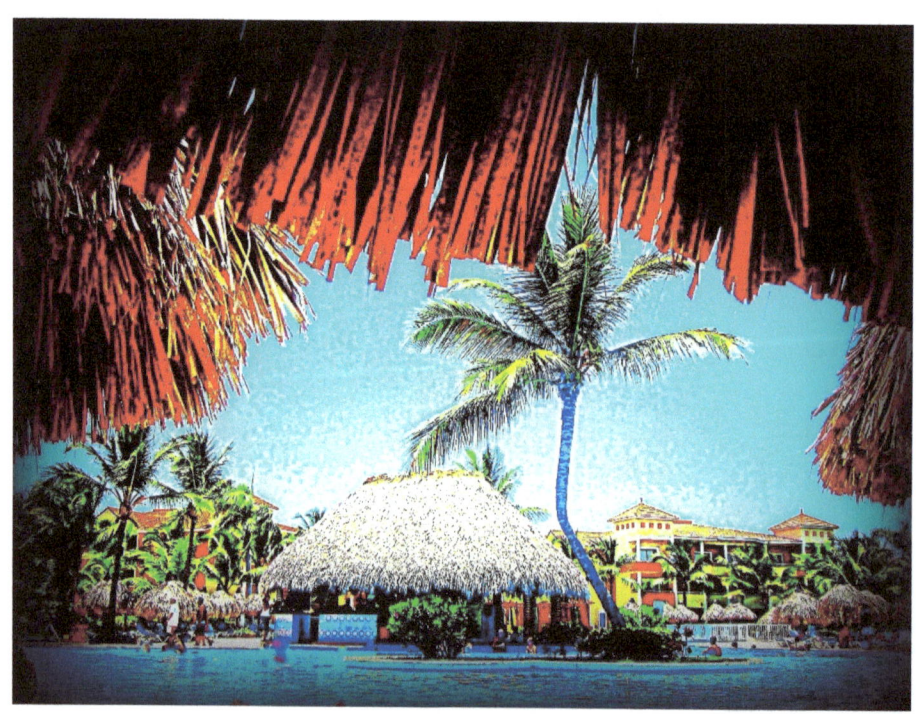

Happy Hour

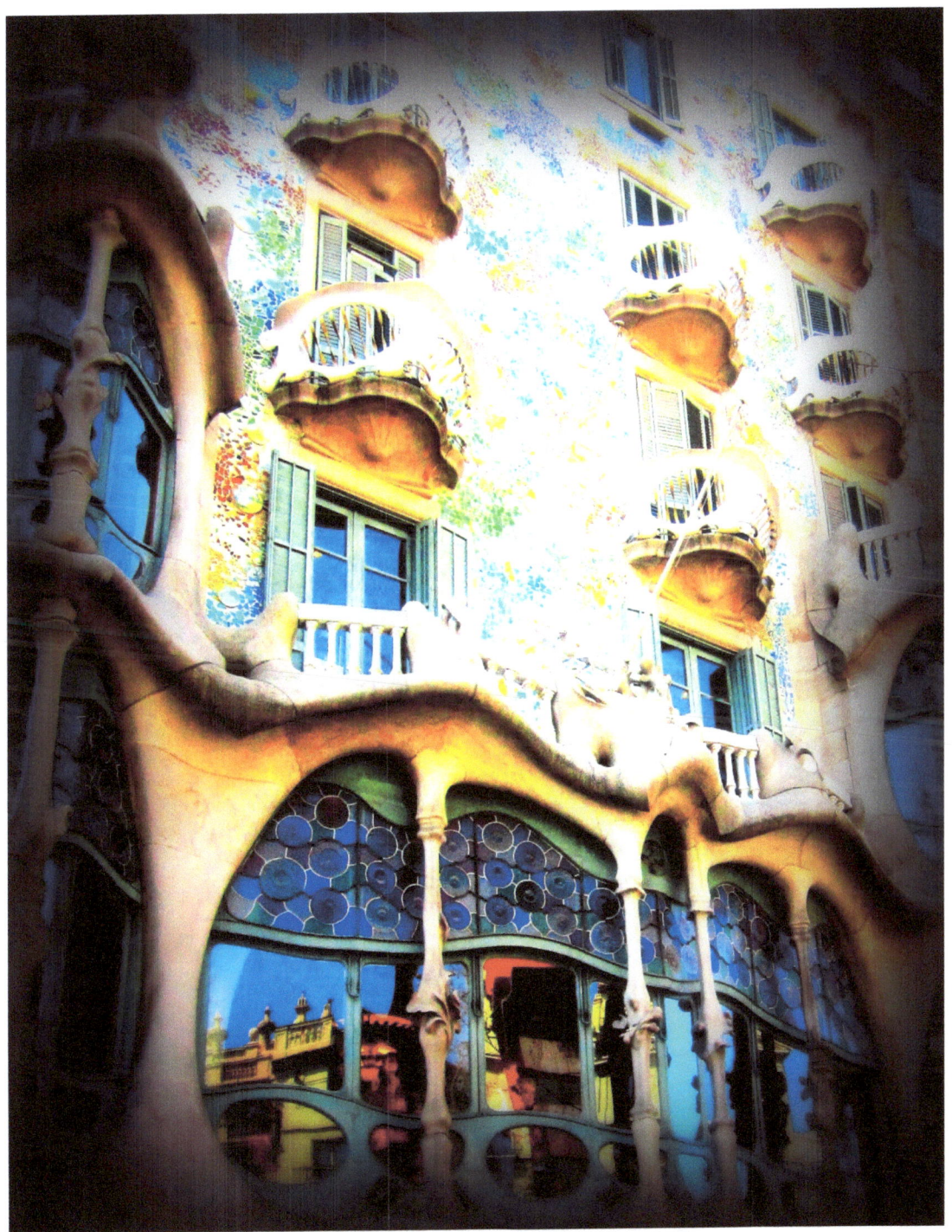

Gaudi, Barcelona

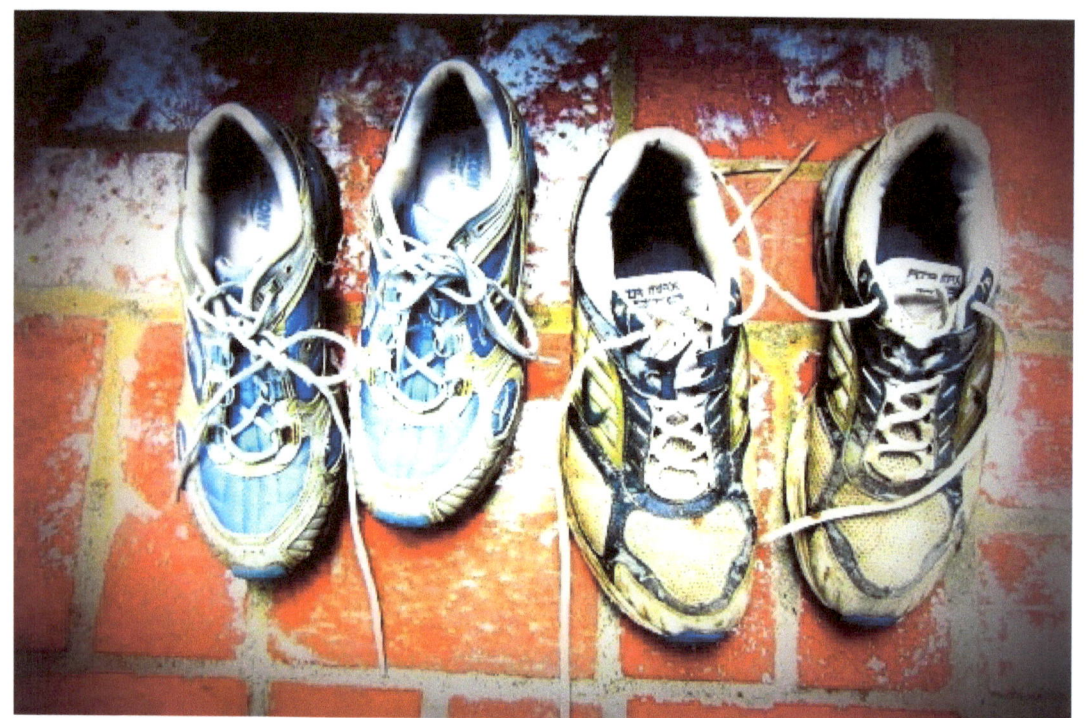

California Joggers

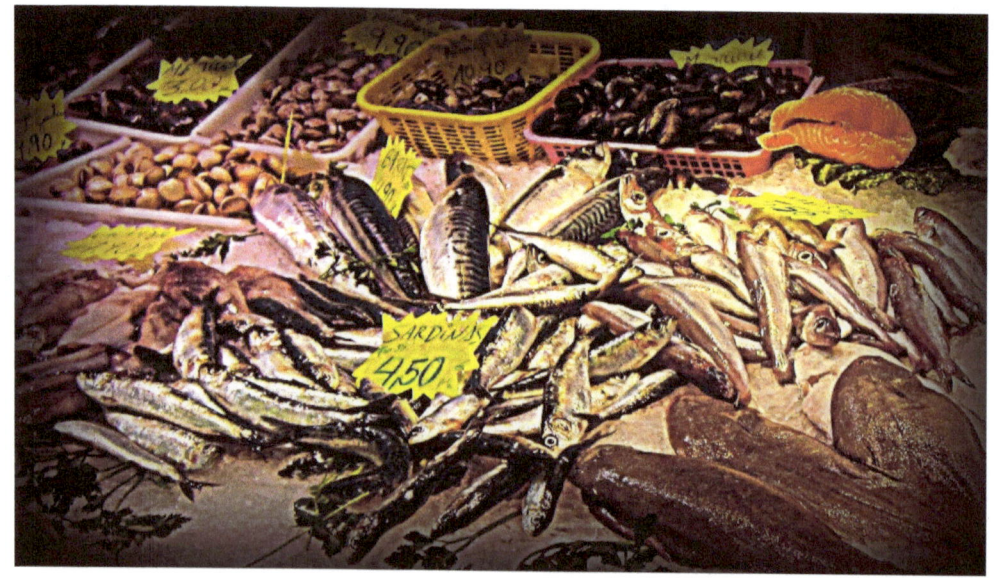

Something a Little Fishy

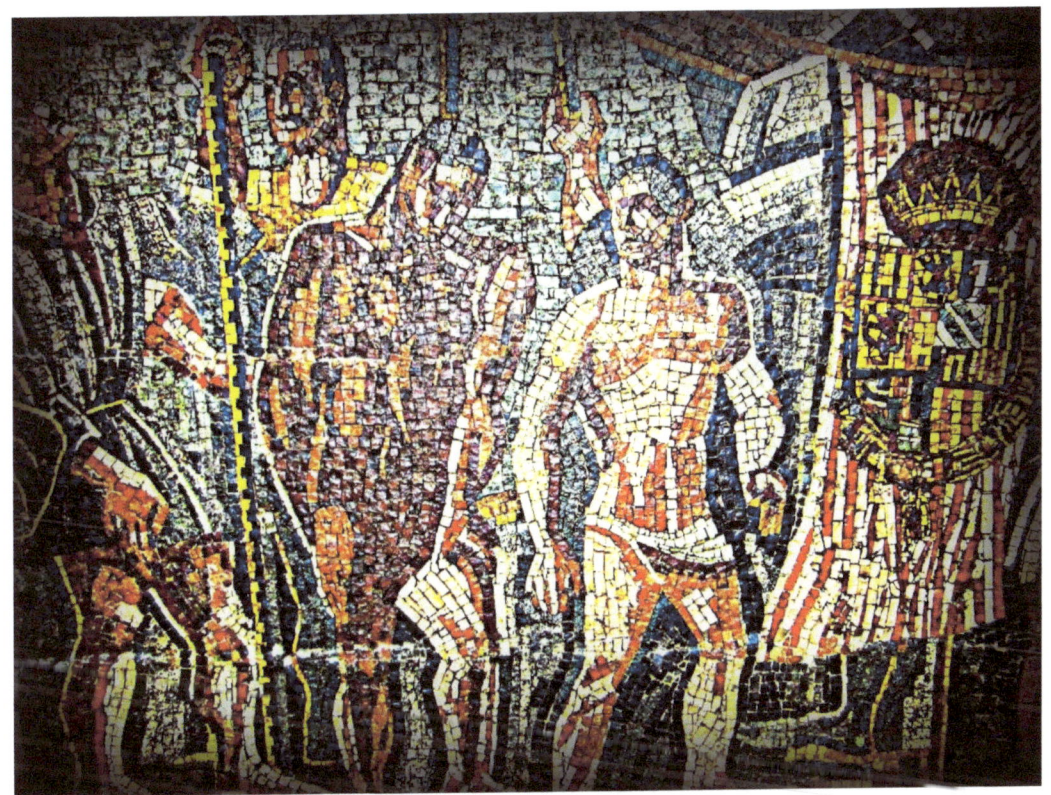

Noble Work

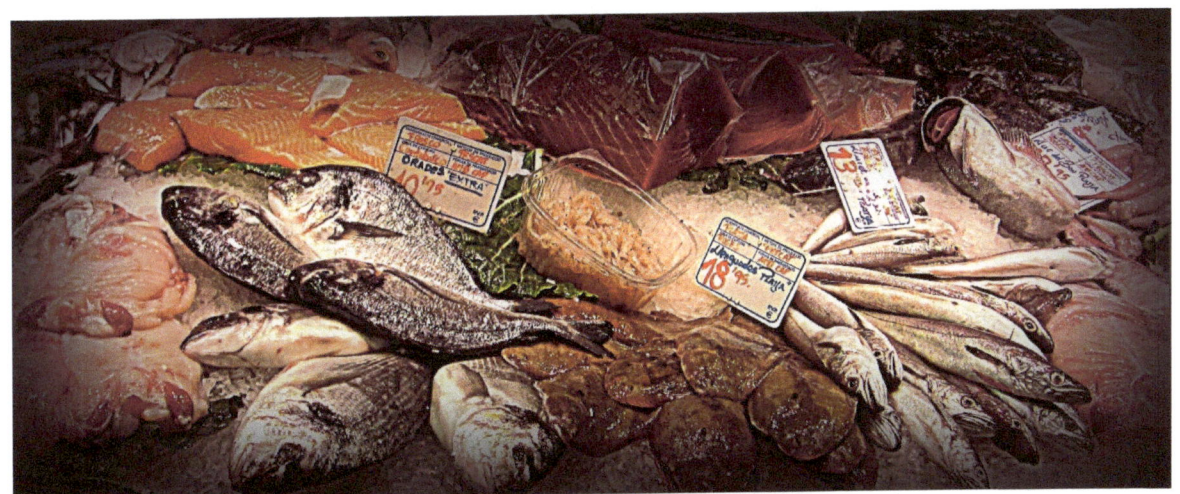

Barcelona Fish Market

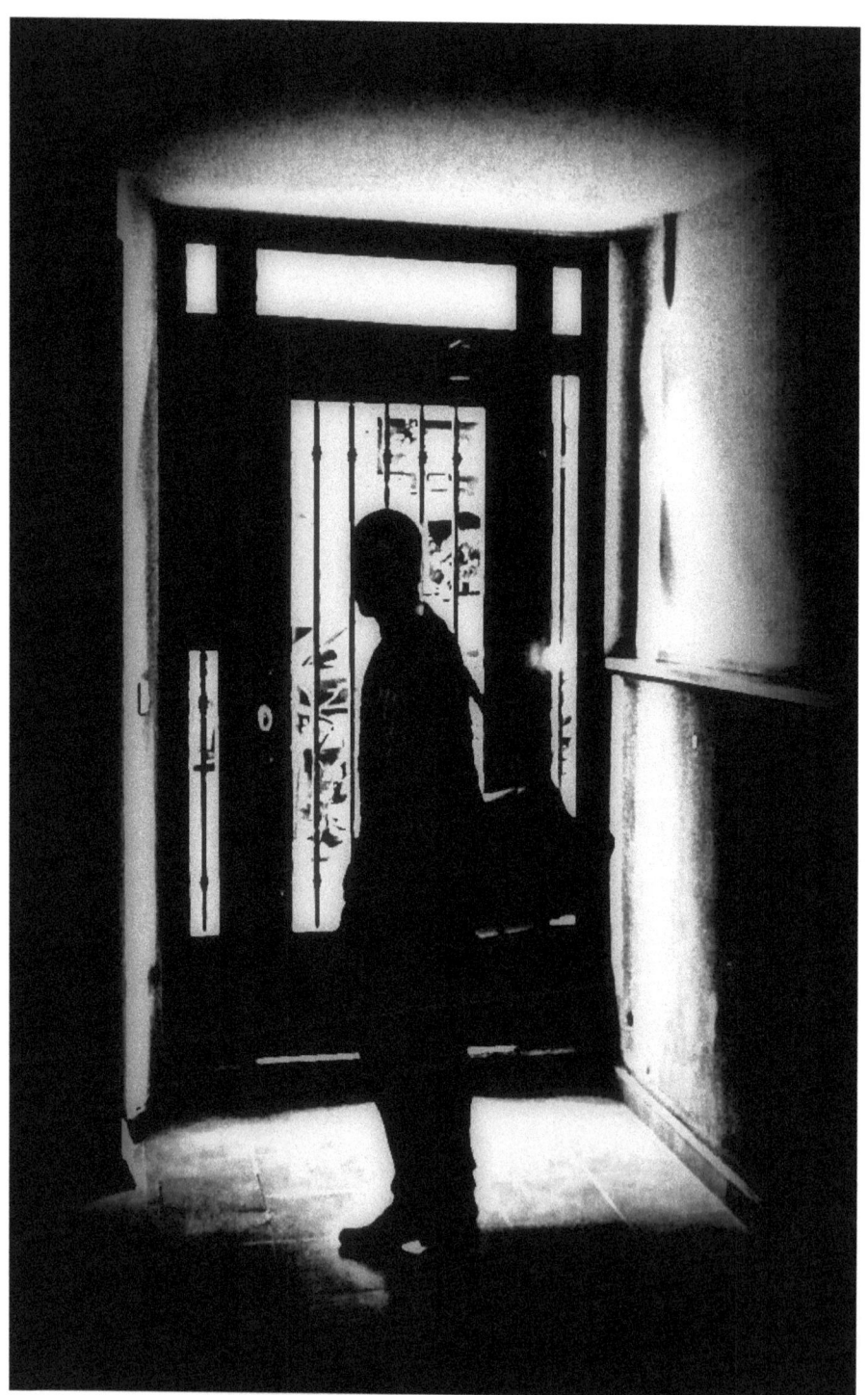

Jack in the Hall, Barcelona

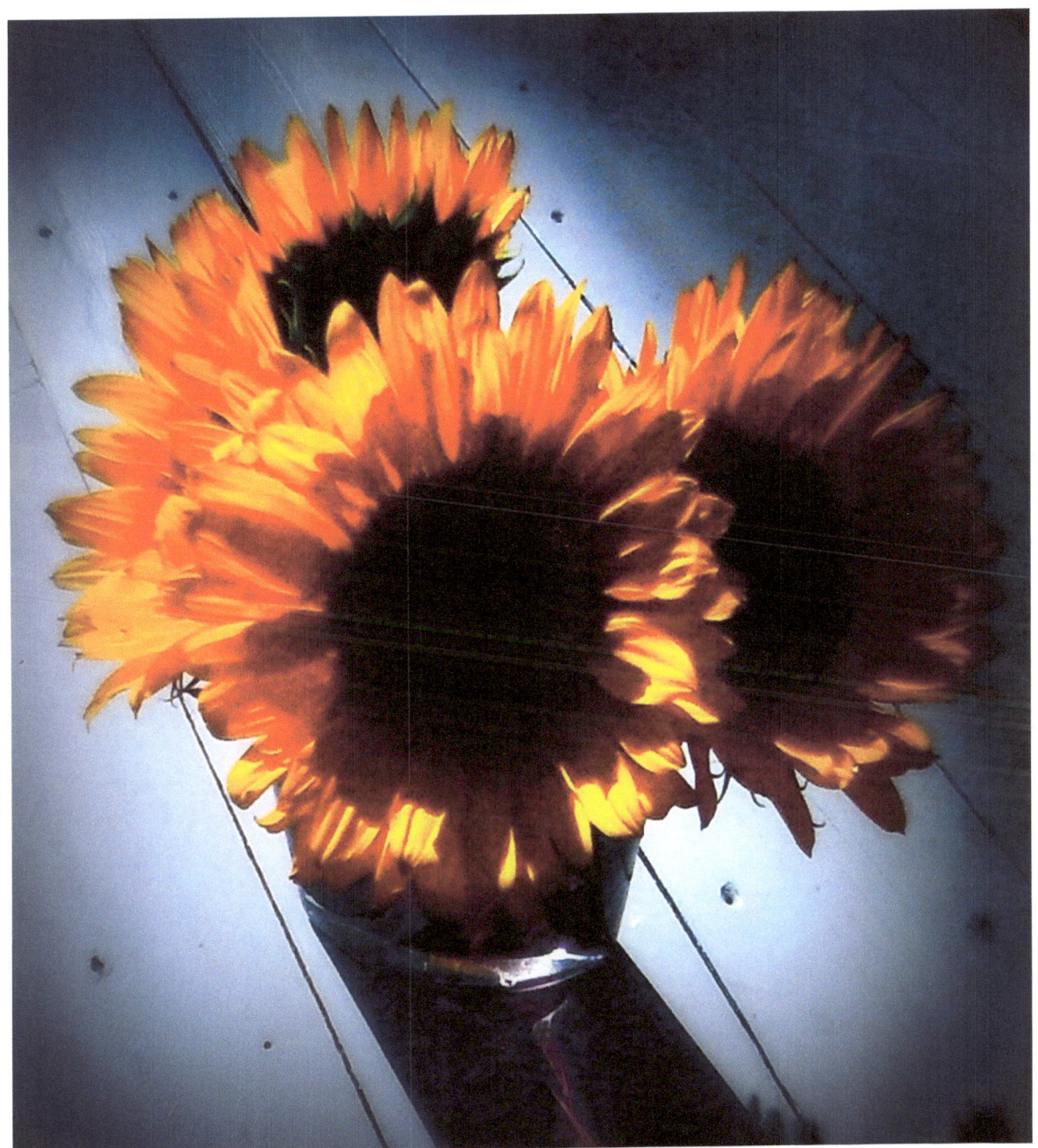

The Other Sunflowers

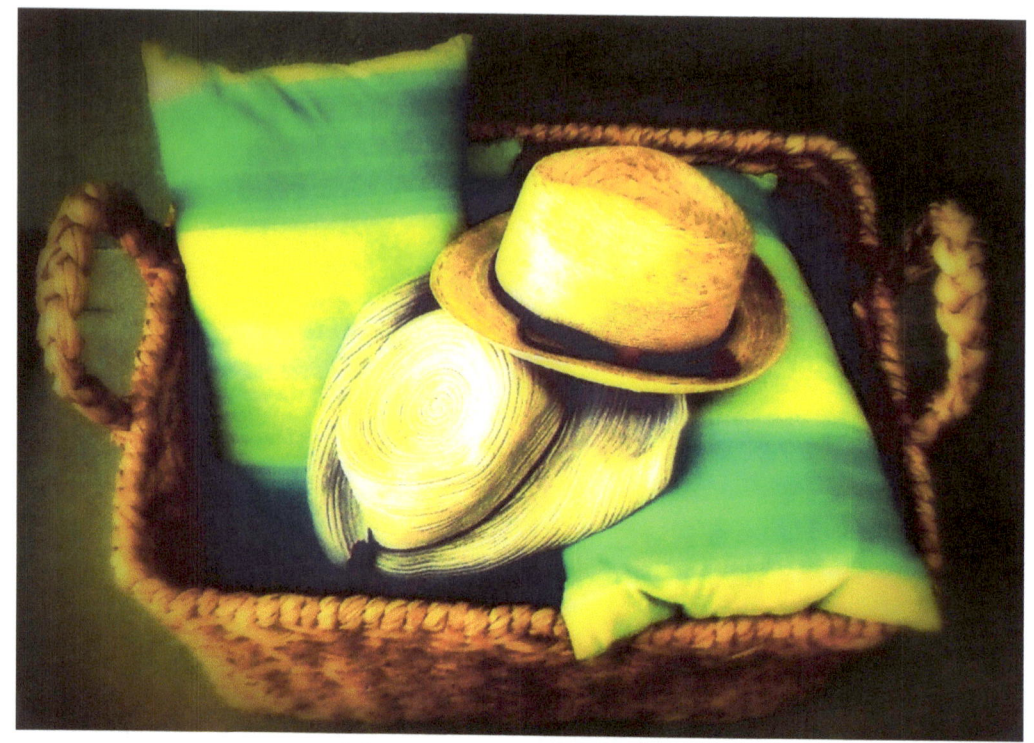

Hats in a Basket

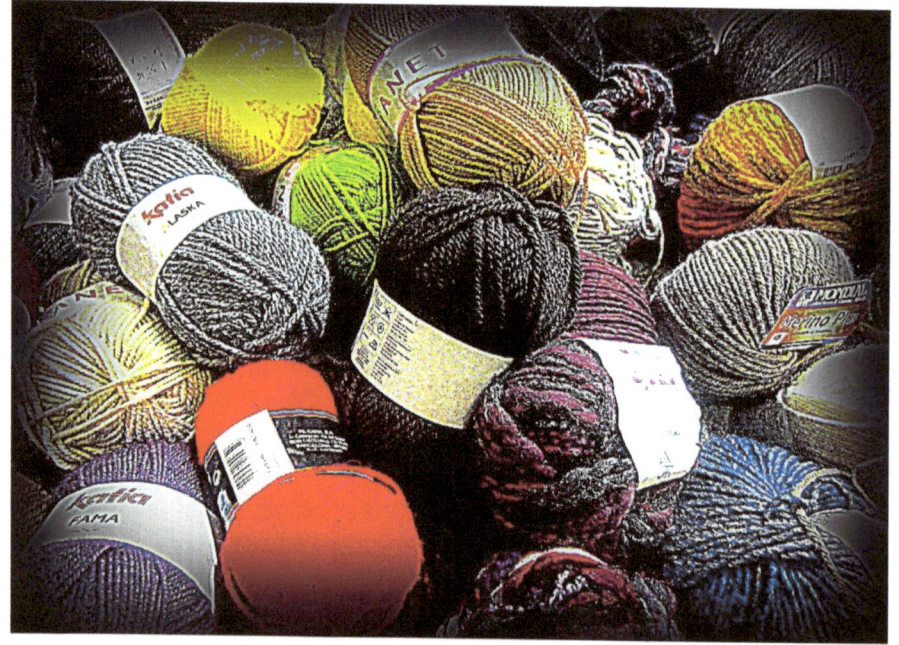

Tall Yarns

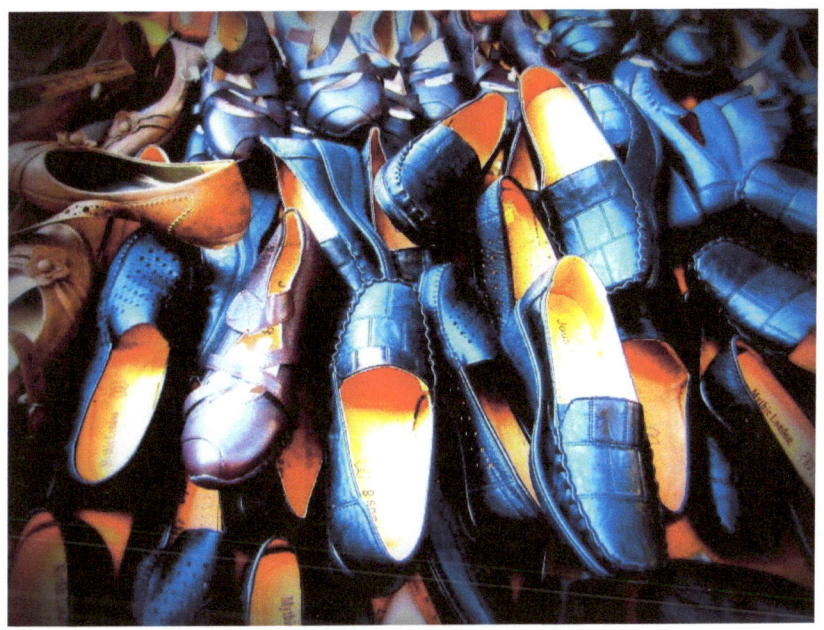

Bless My Sole

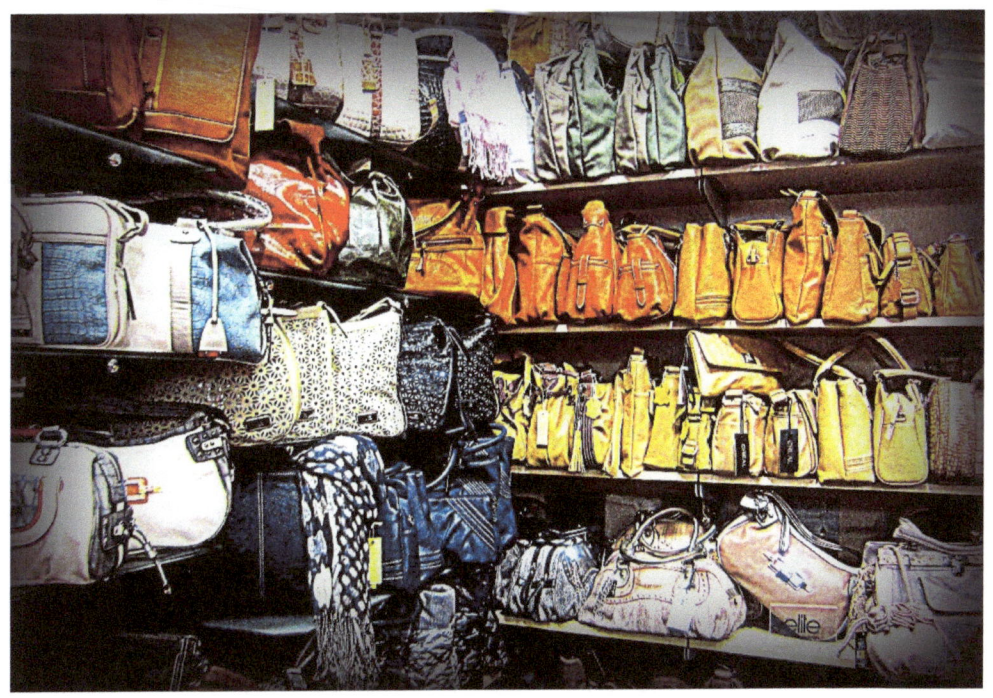

Out of the Bag

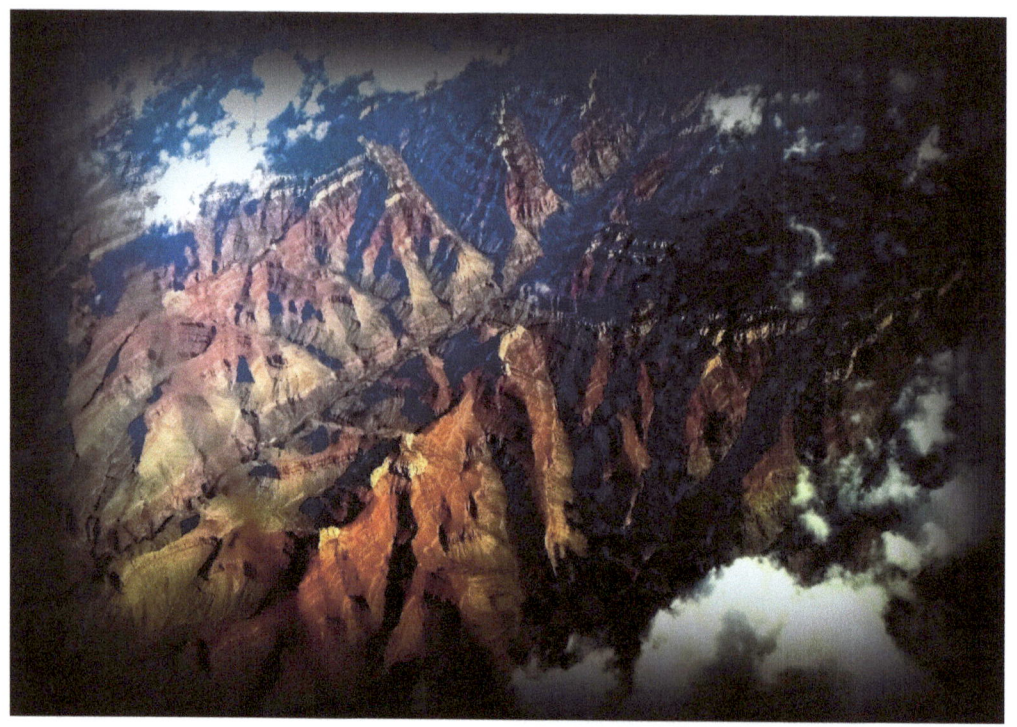

Grand Canyon I

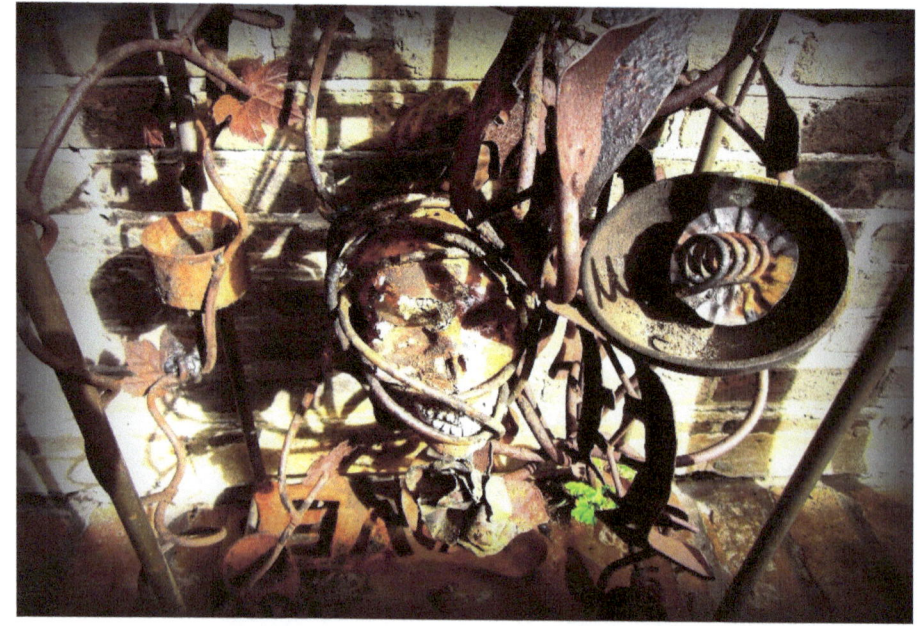

Santa Barbara Wall

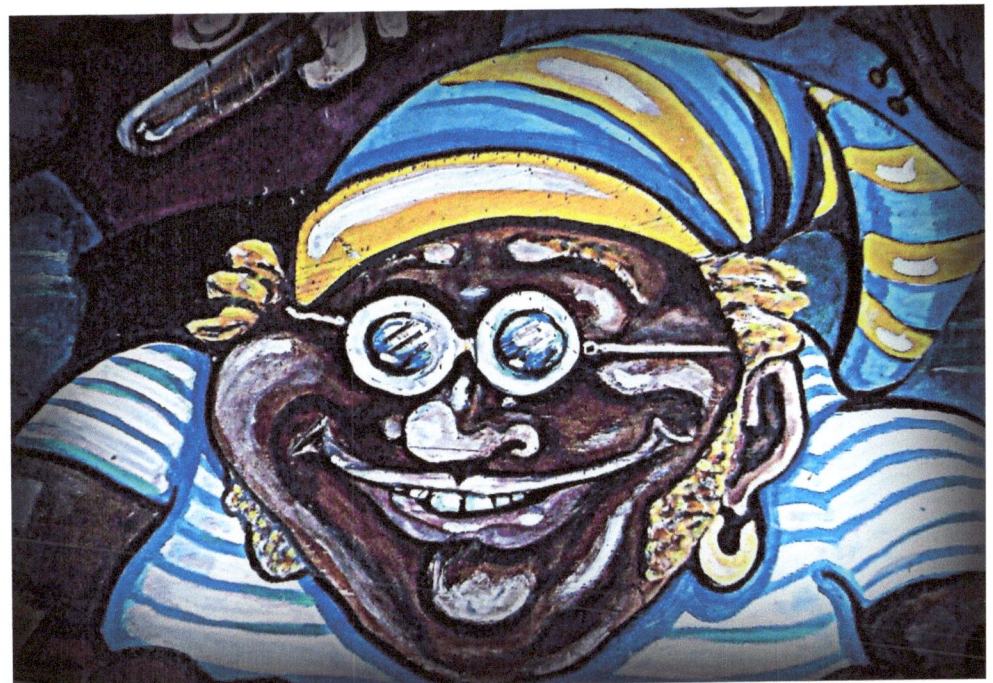

Bahama Mama

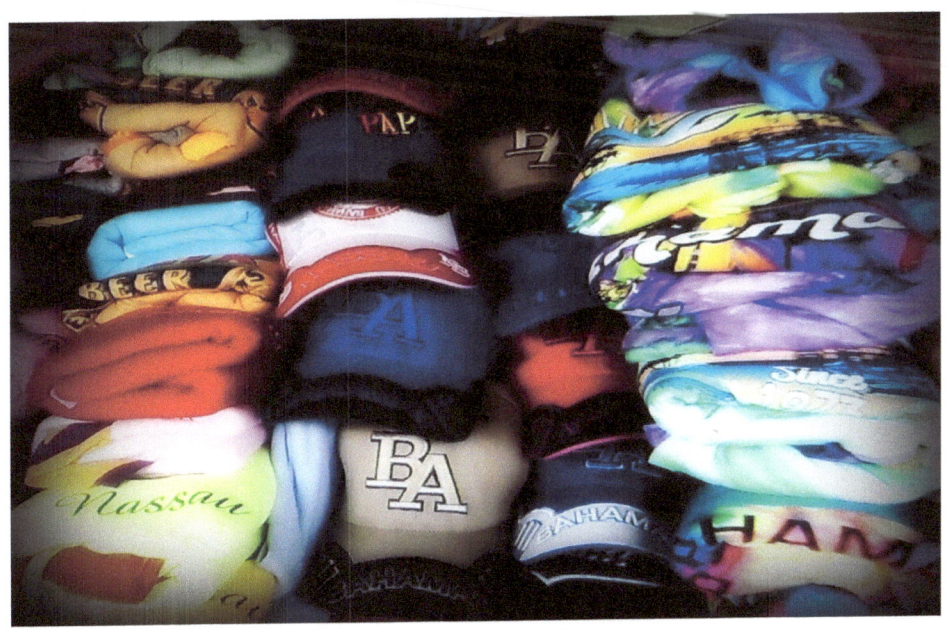

Getting Shirty

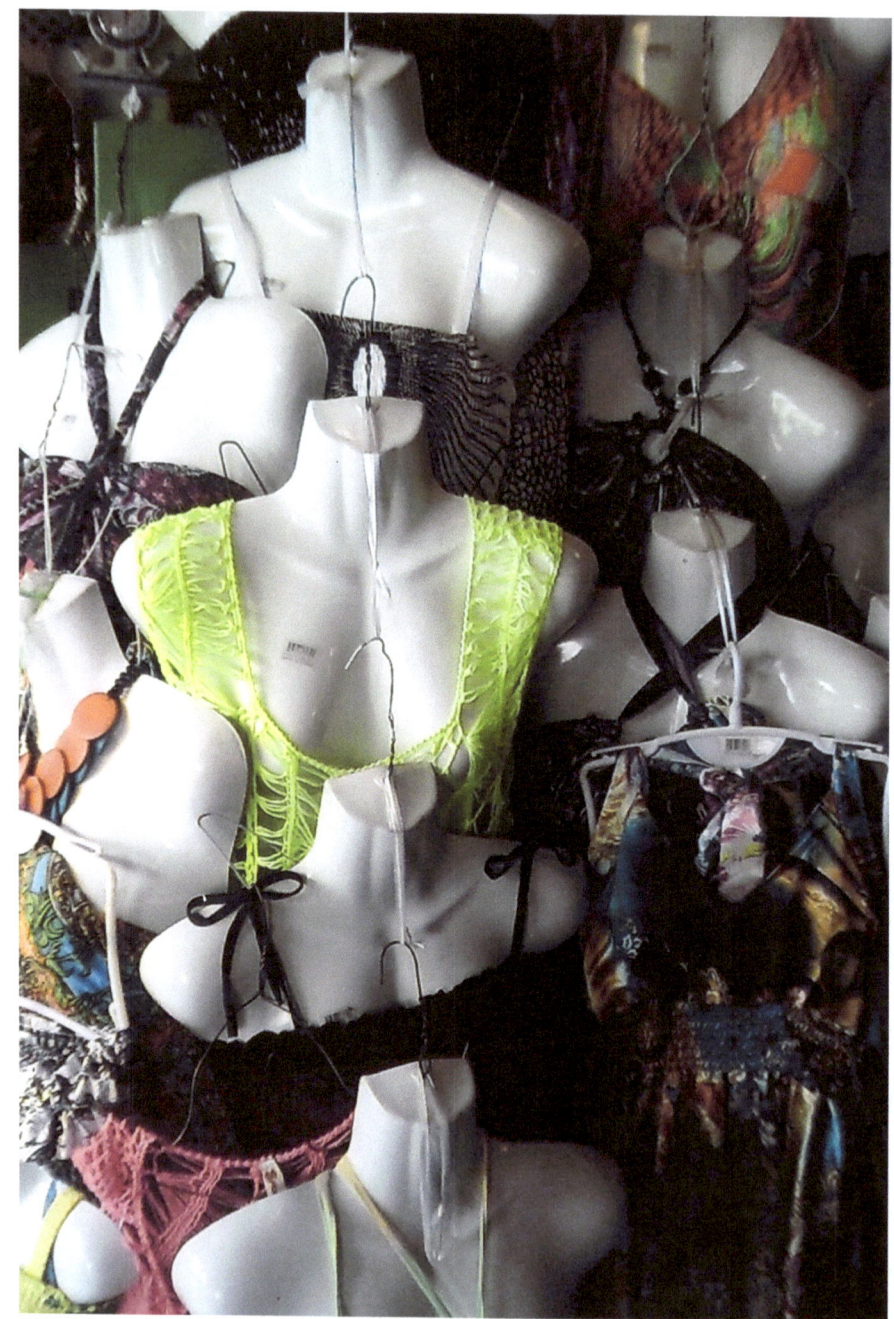

The Brass Section

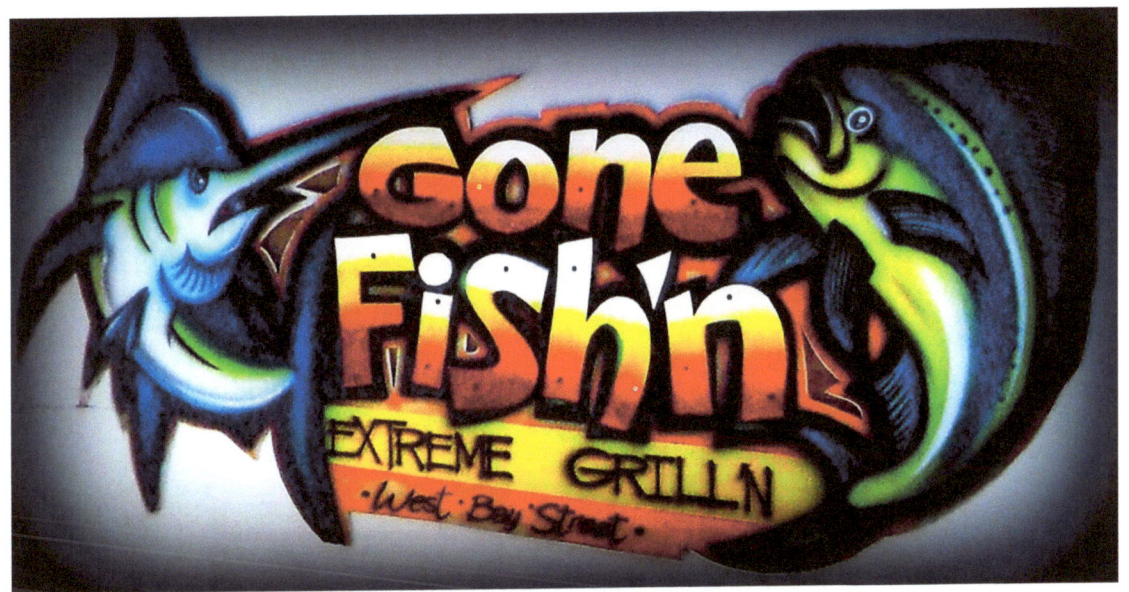

If Only...

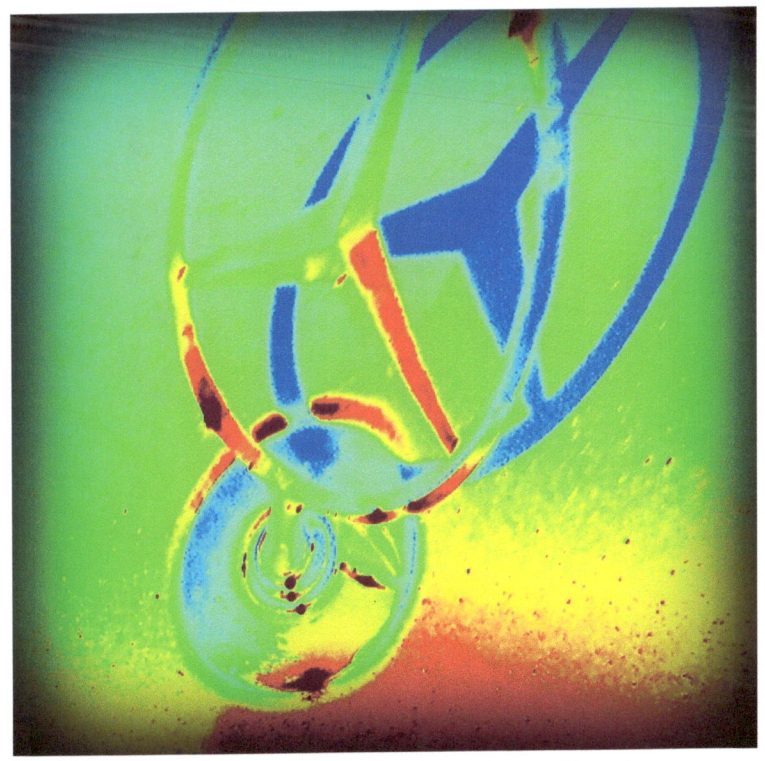

Mercedez Bends the Rules

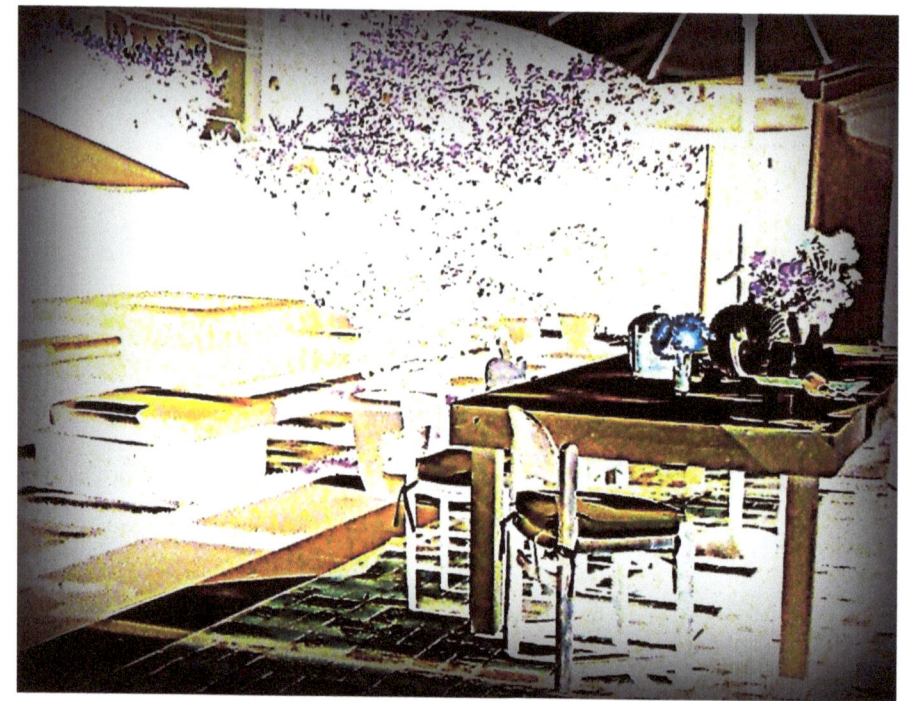

Studio City by the Pool

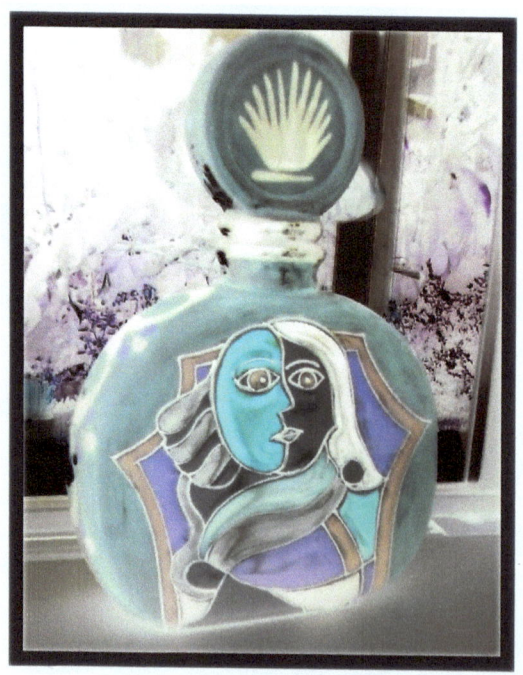

Vase Deferens

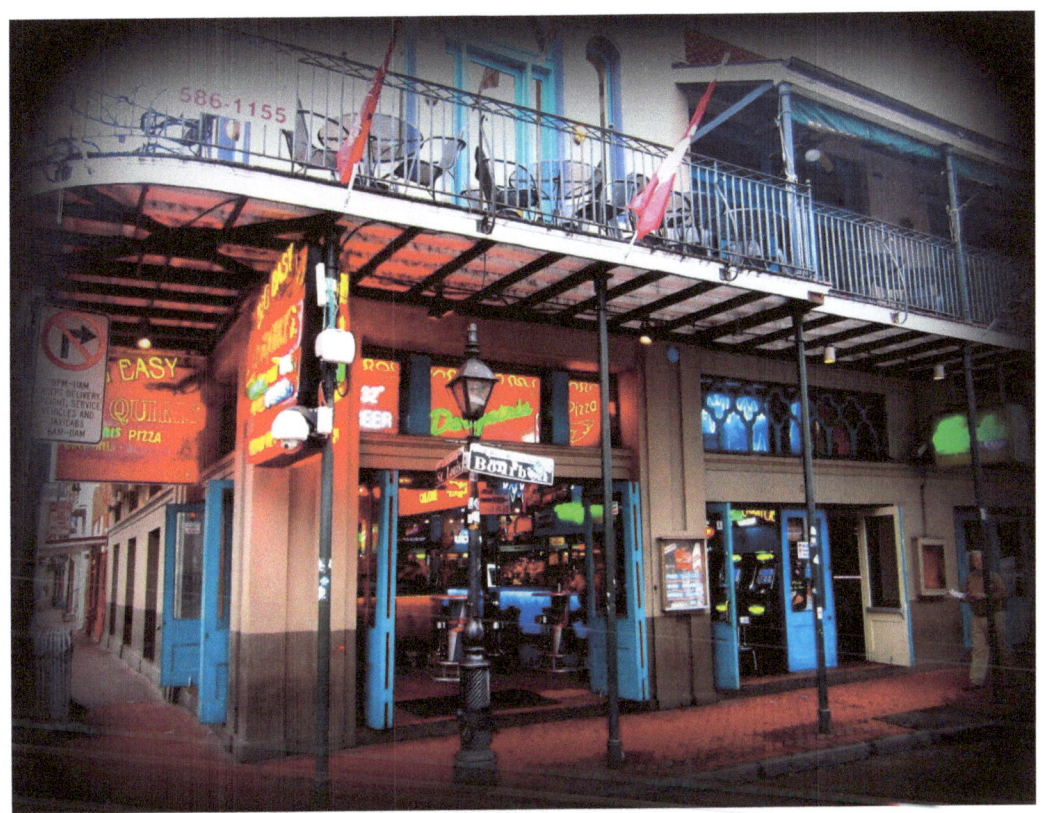

Bourbon Street

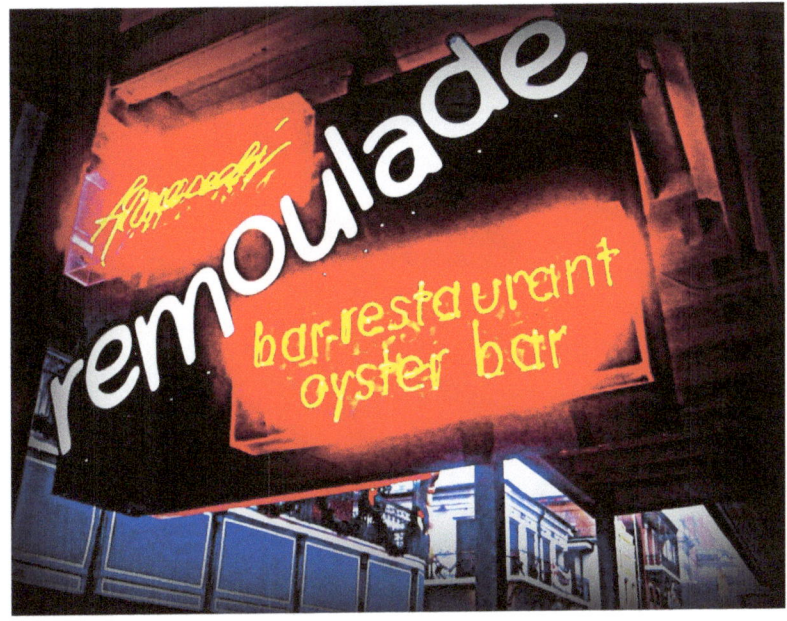

Oysters on Bourbon Street

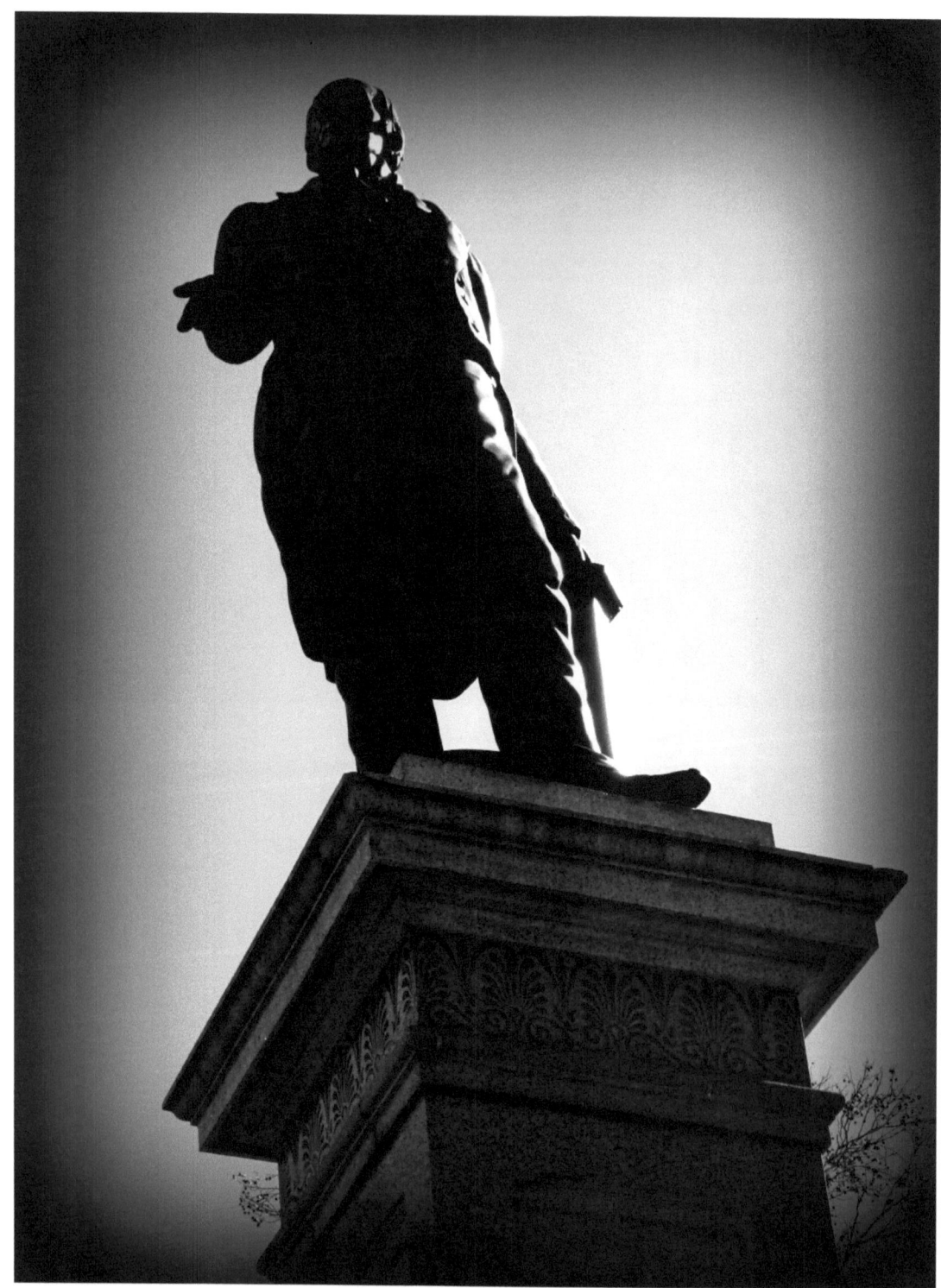

Important Fellow

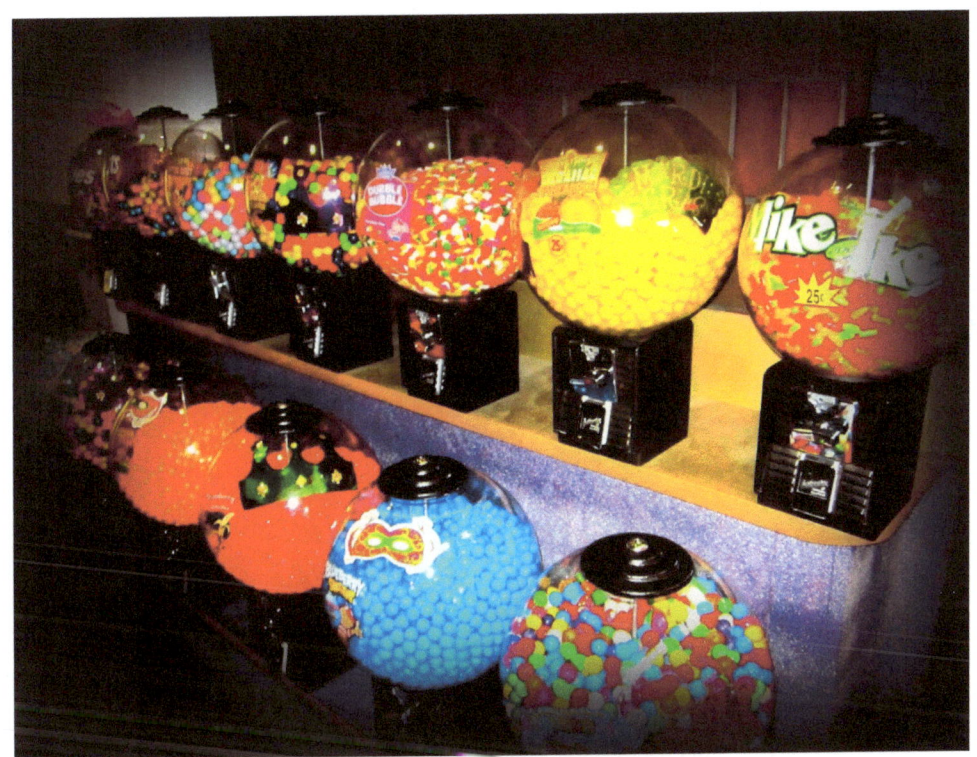

Eye Candy

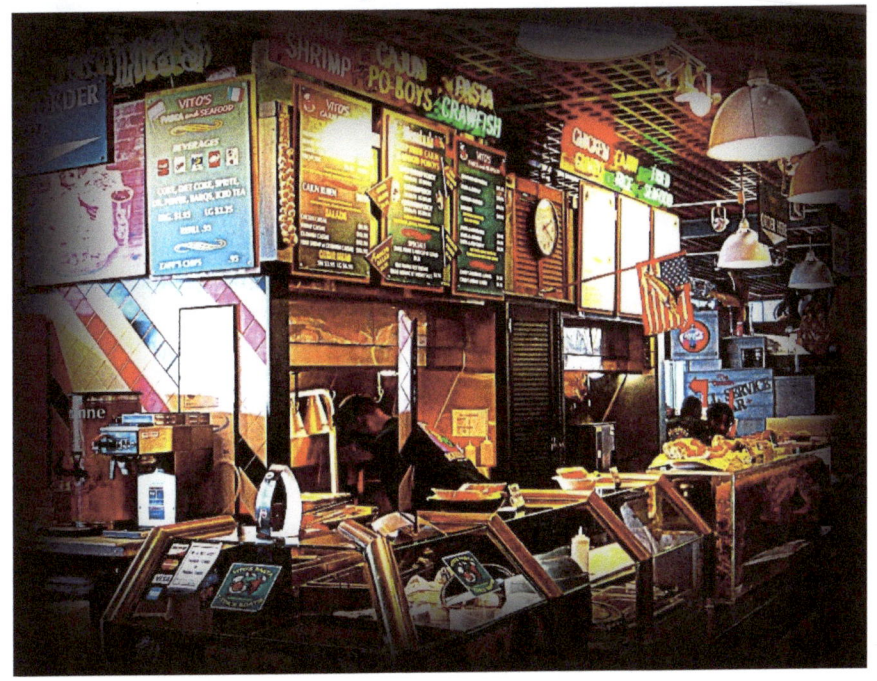

Snacks in New Orleans

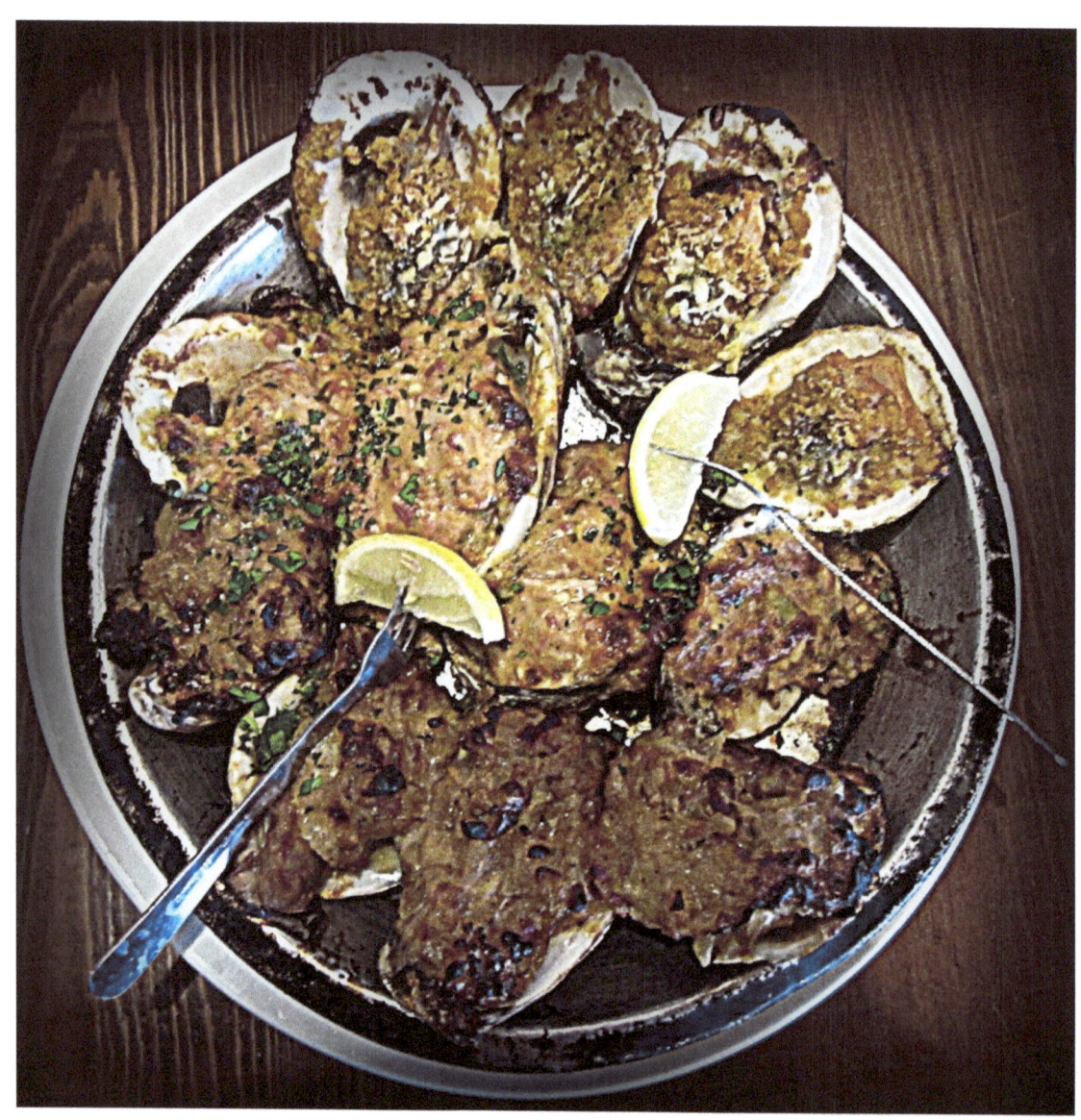

Twelve of the Best!
Oyster Bar – New Orleans

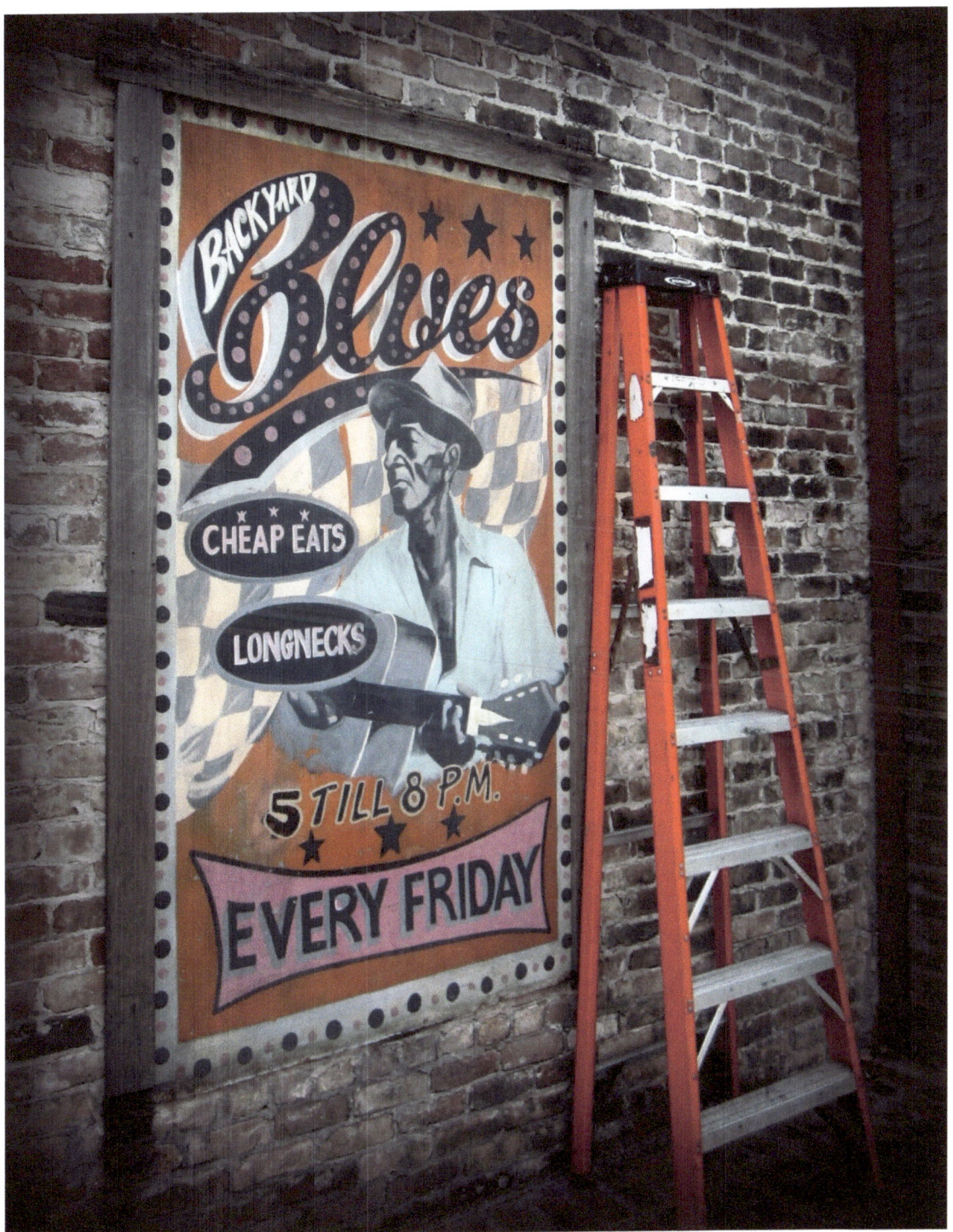

Backyard Blues

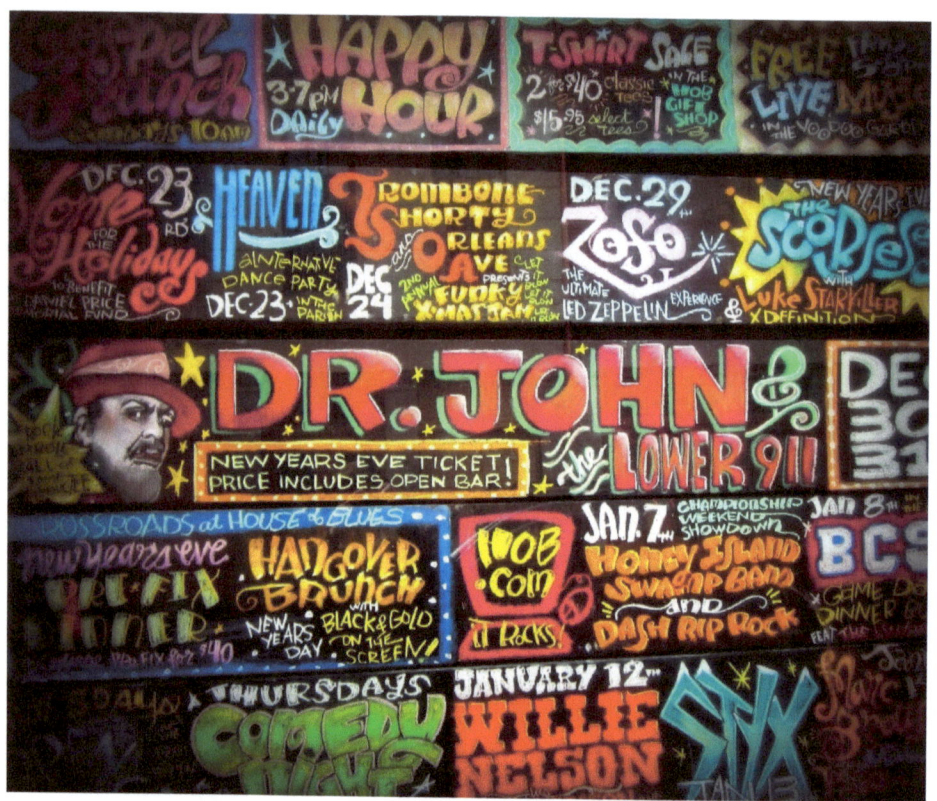

House of Blues

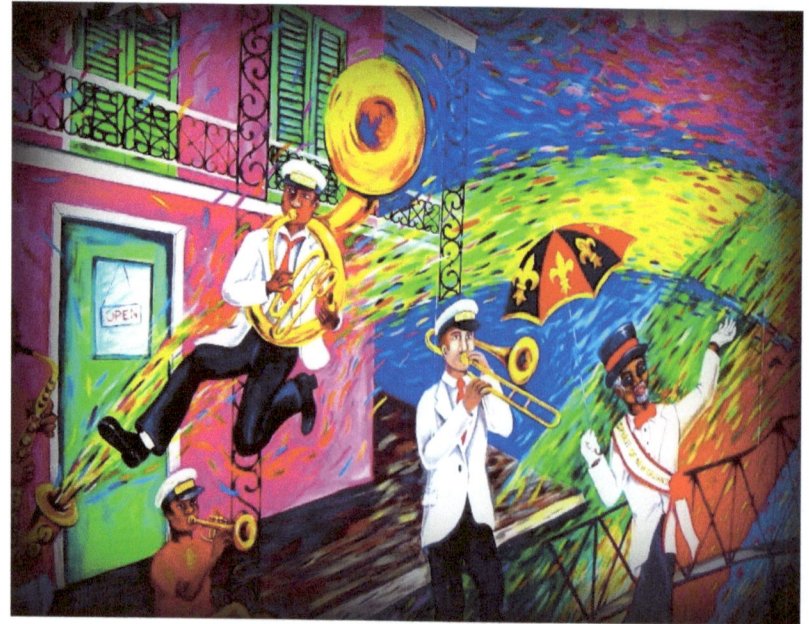

Jazzing it Up

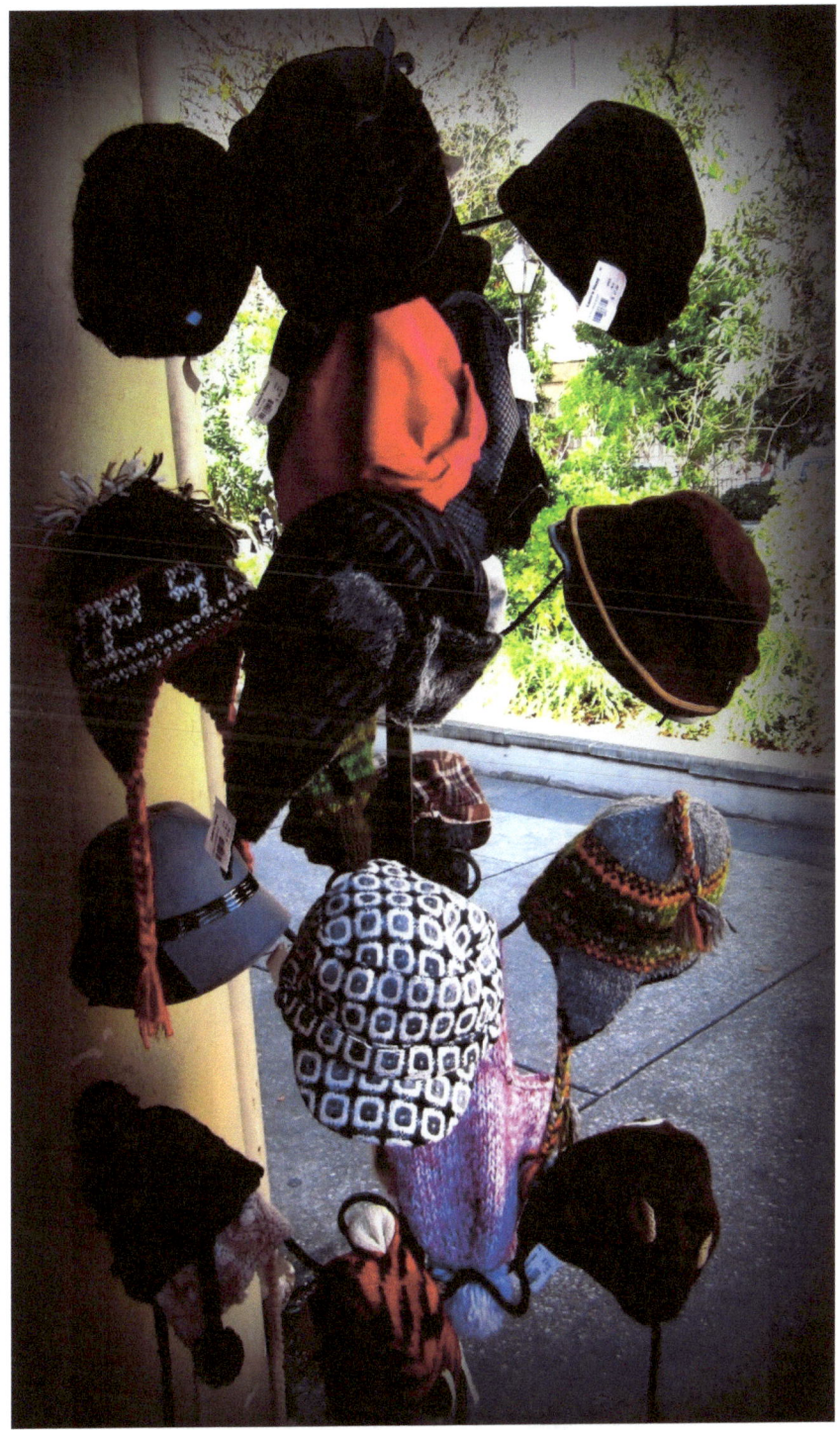

Mad Hatters

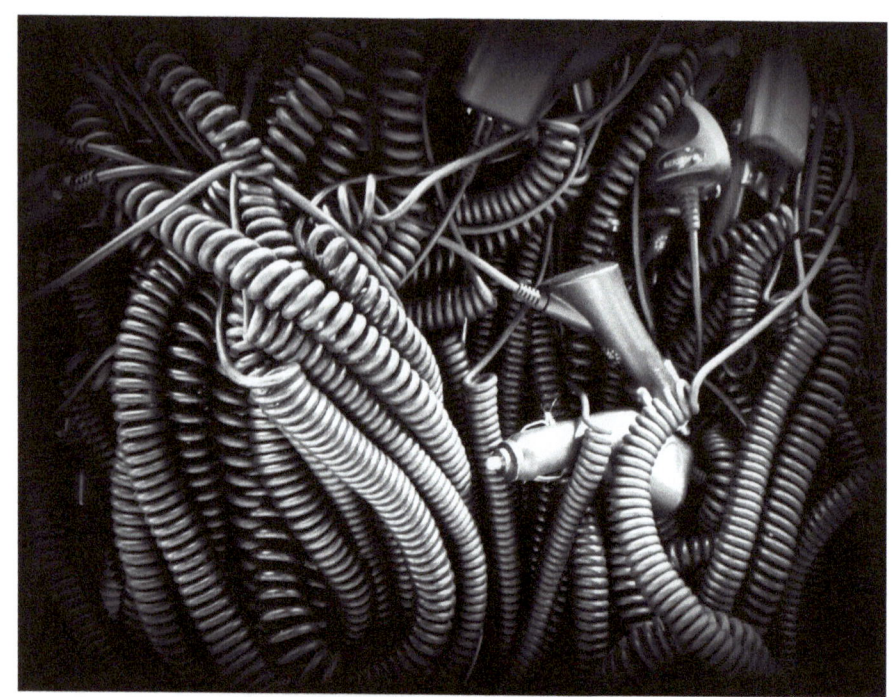

Getting Wired

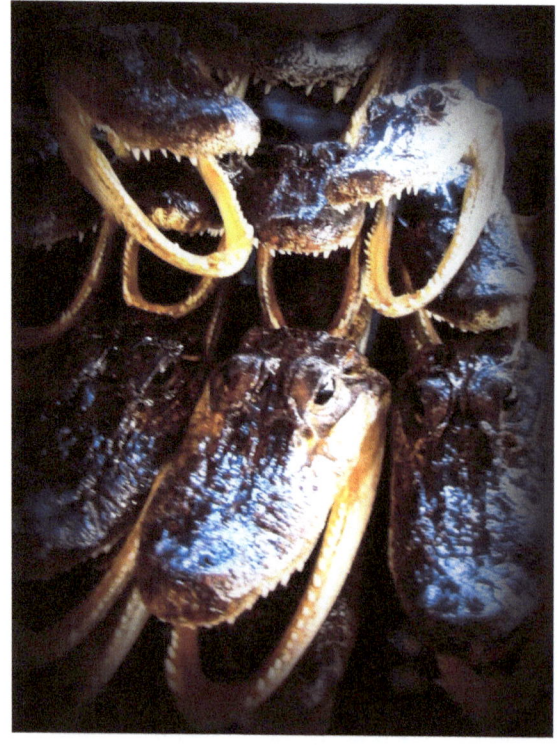

IRS

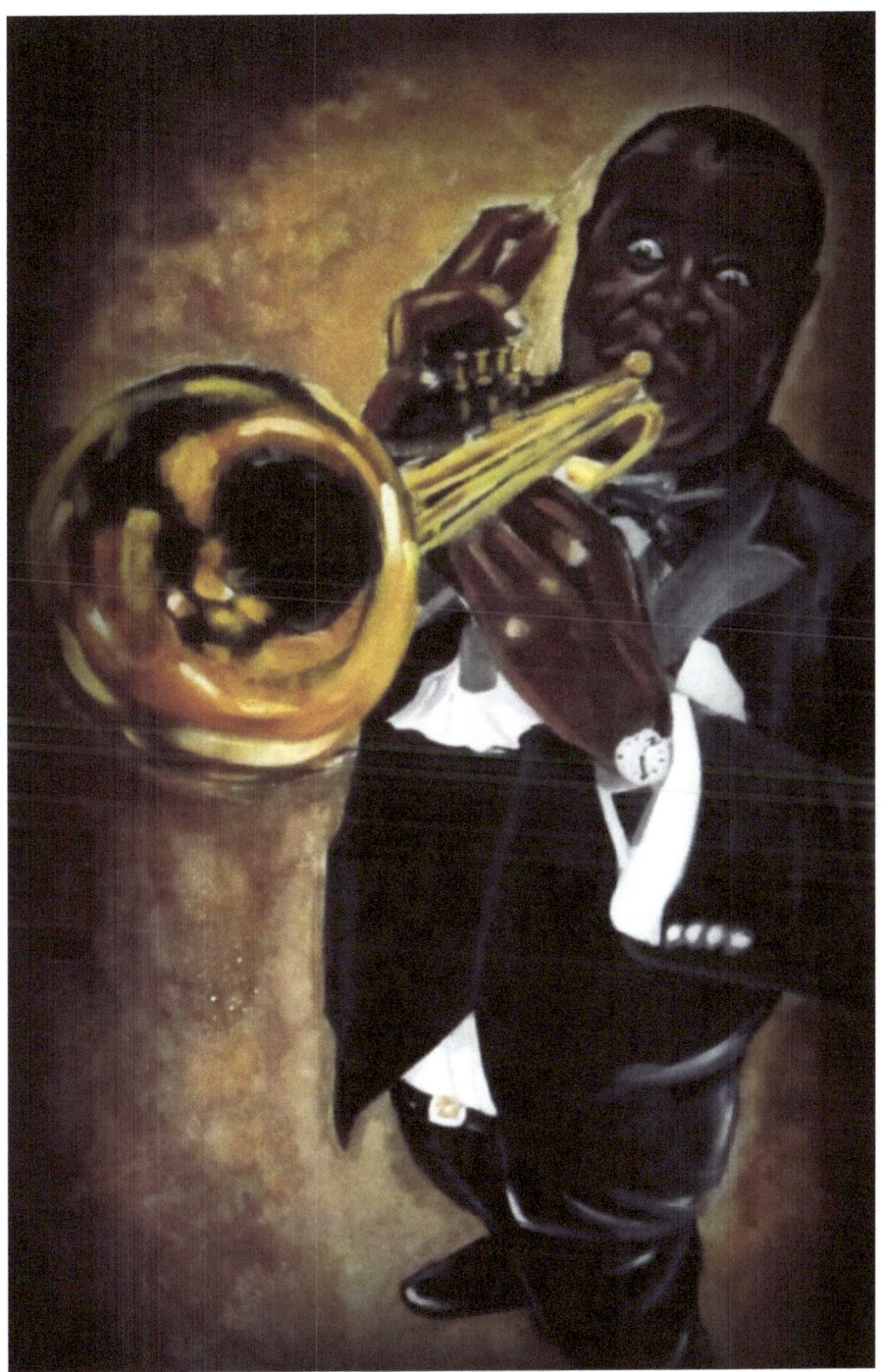

Satchmo

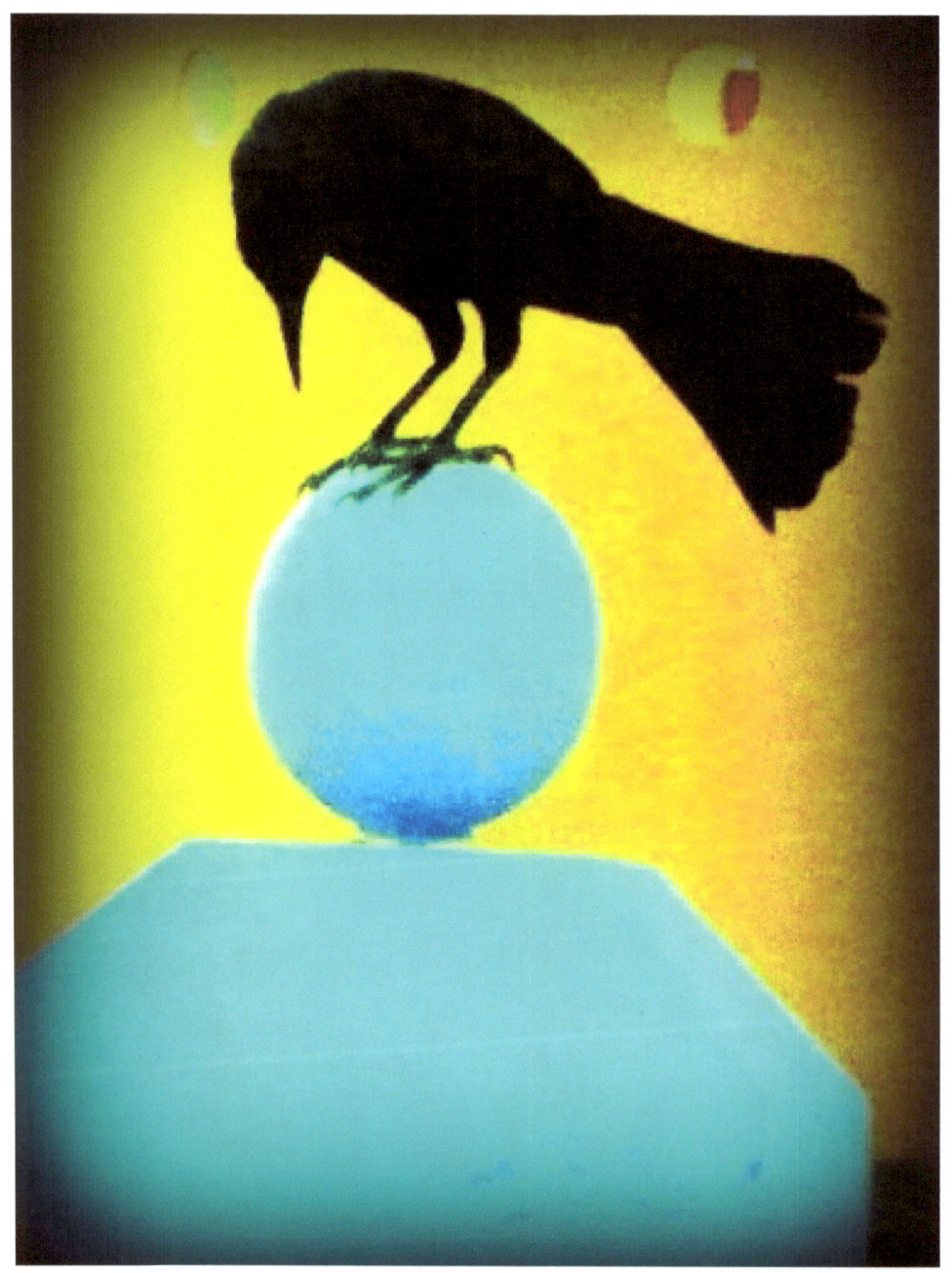

Surreal Poe Boy

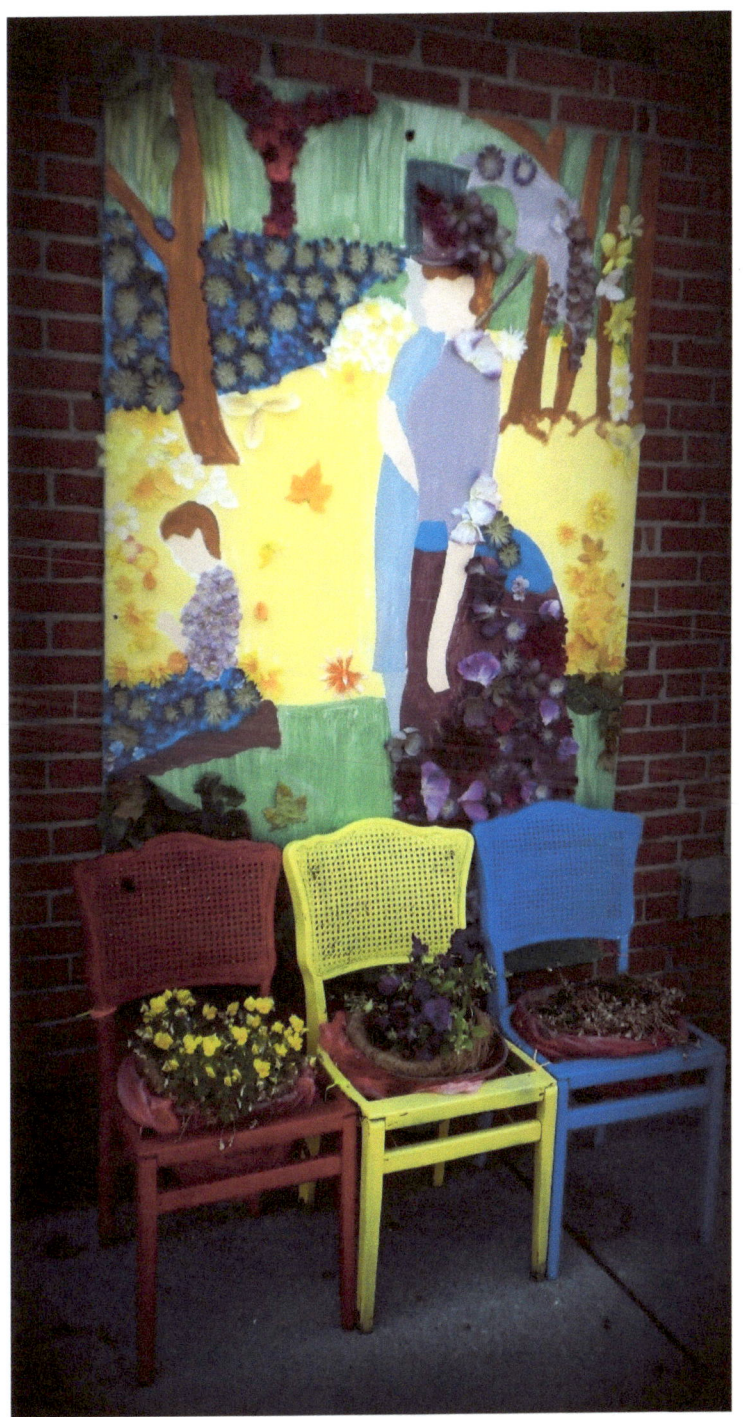

Westerville, Oh. – Wall and Chairs

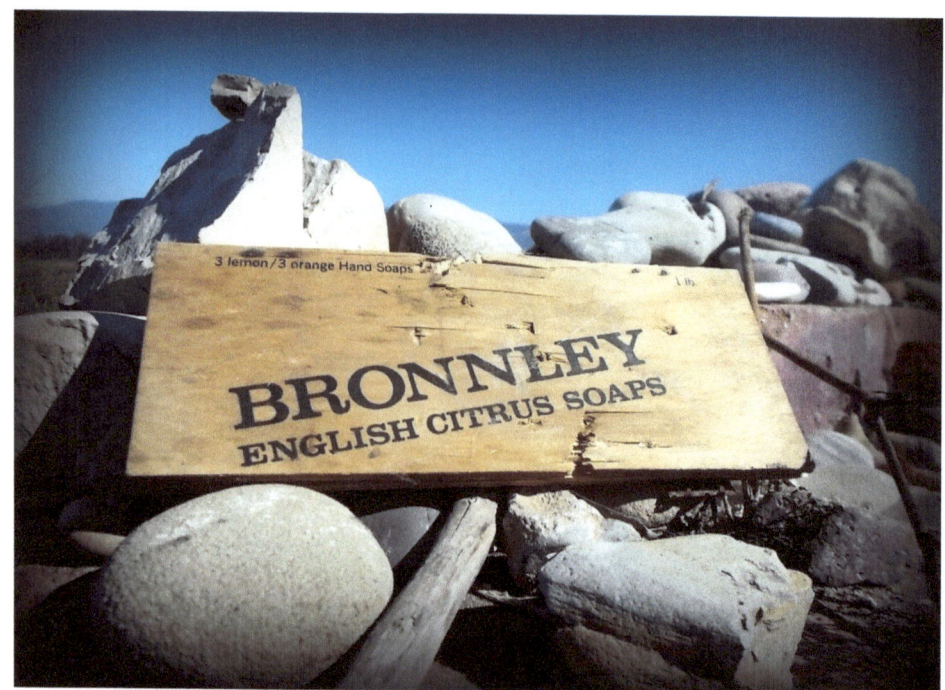

Cleaning Up in Santa Barbara

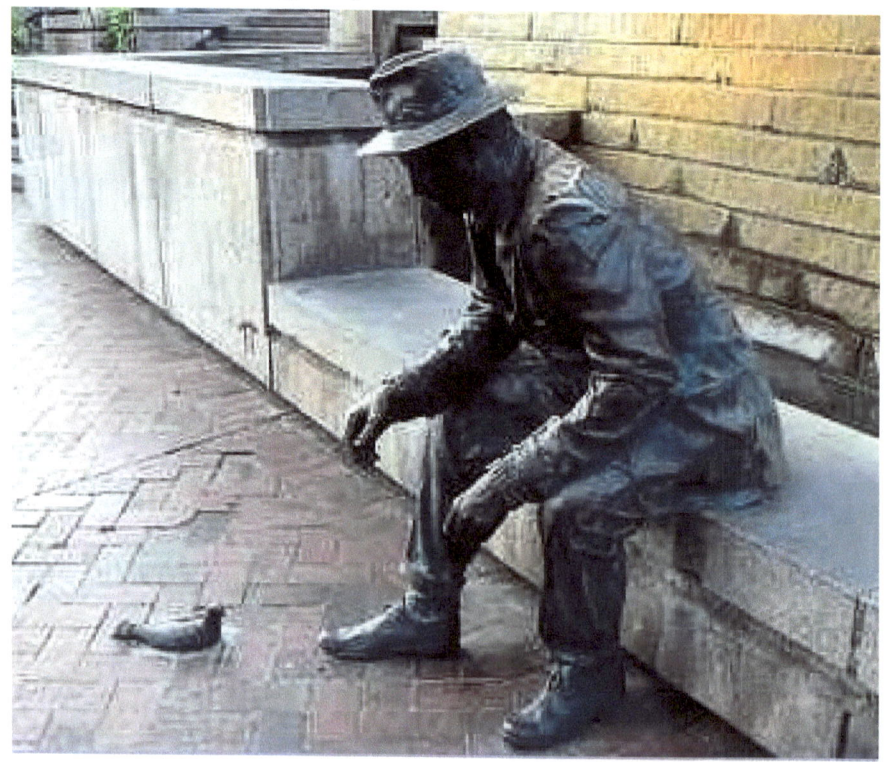

A Slow Day

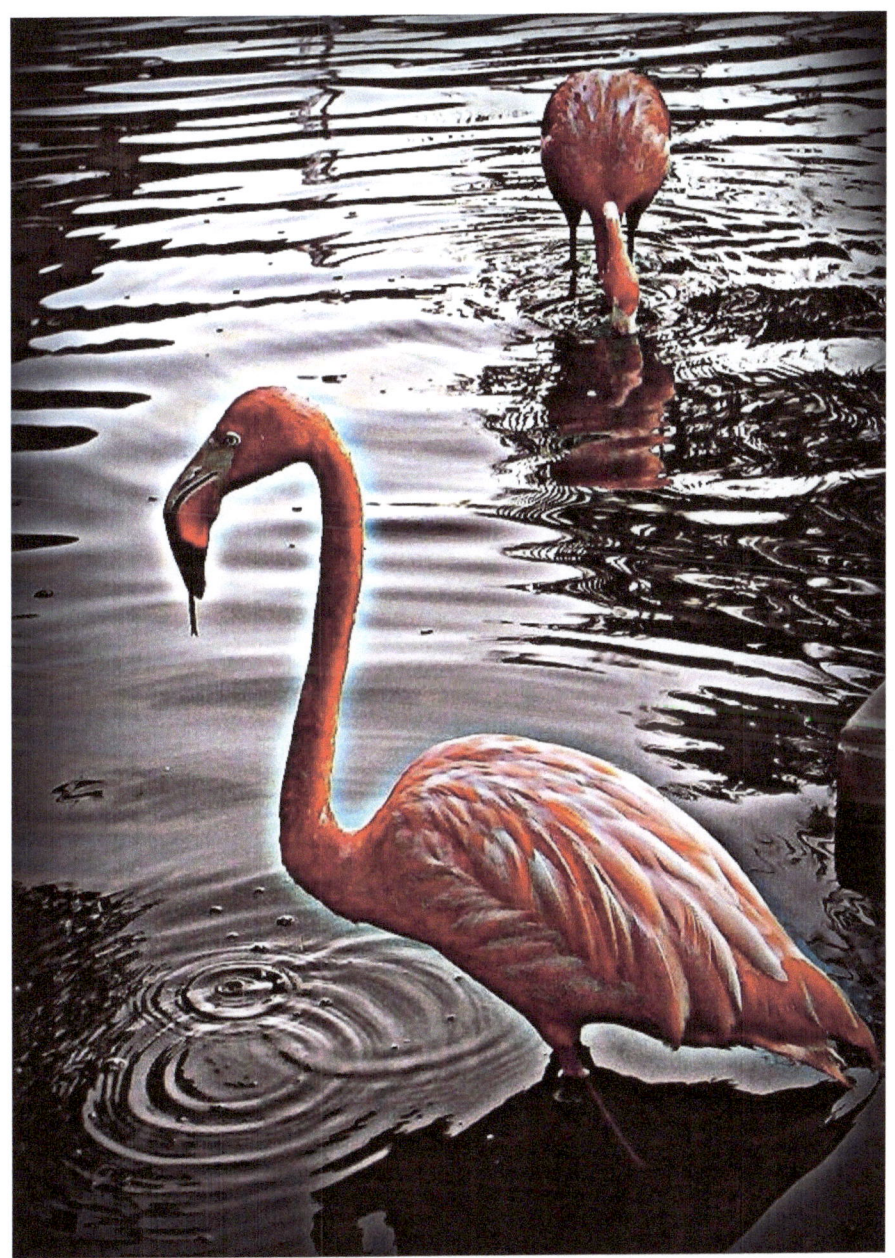

"Moi, a Cliché?"

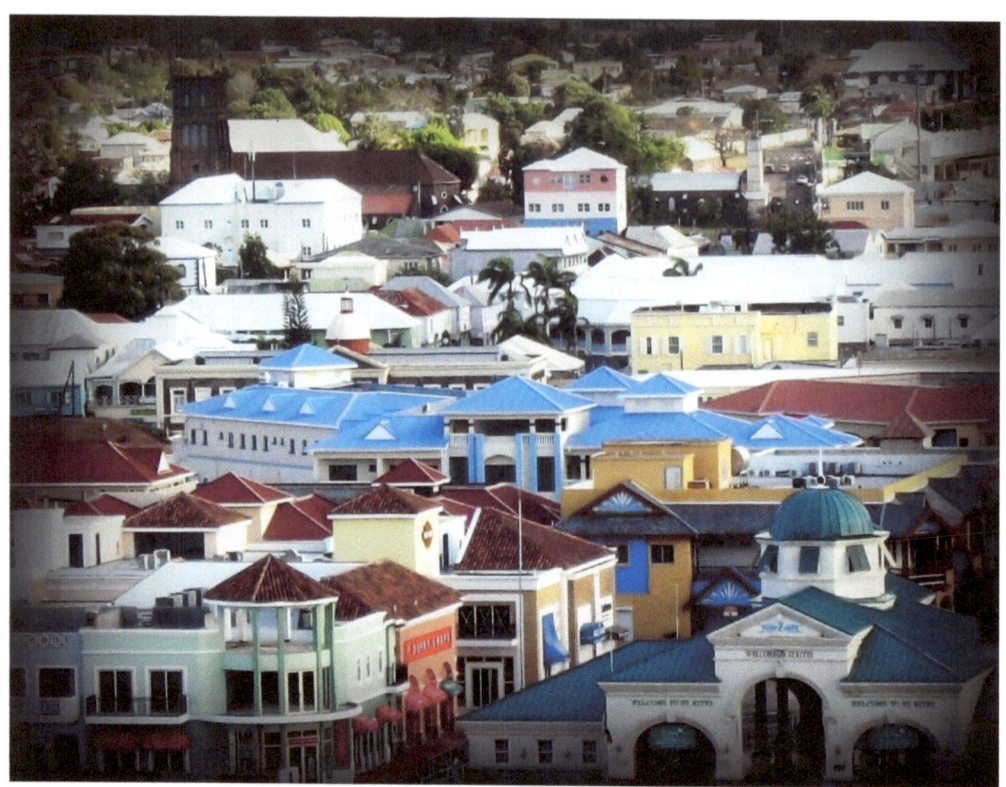

St. Lucia's Harbor Area

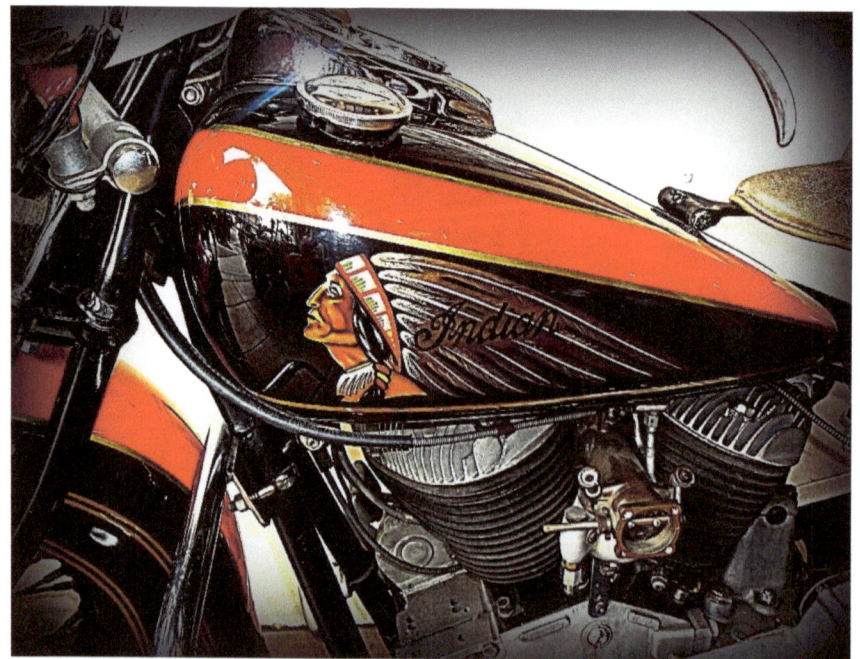

A Friendly Indian

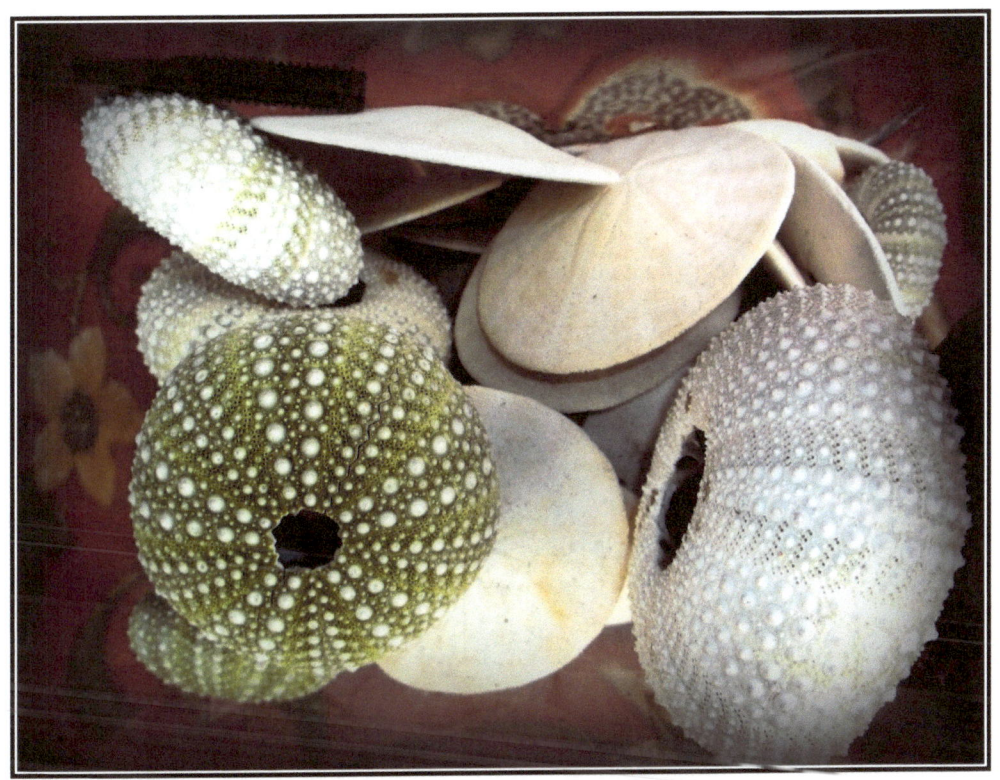

"I see sea shells..."

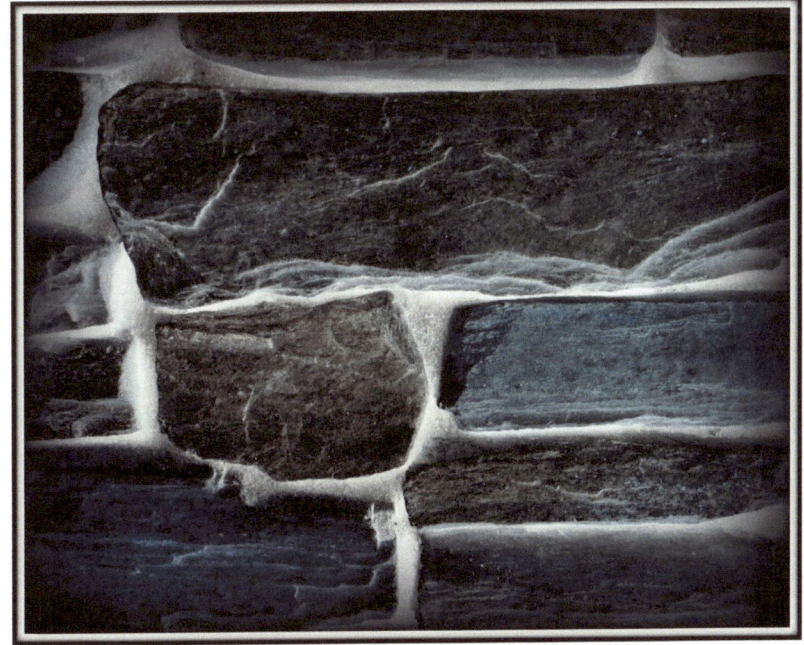

Back to the Wall

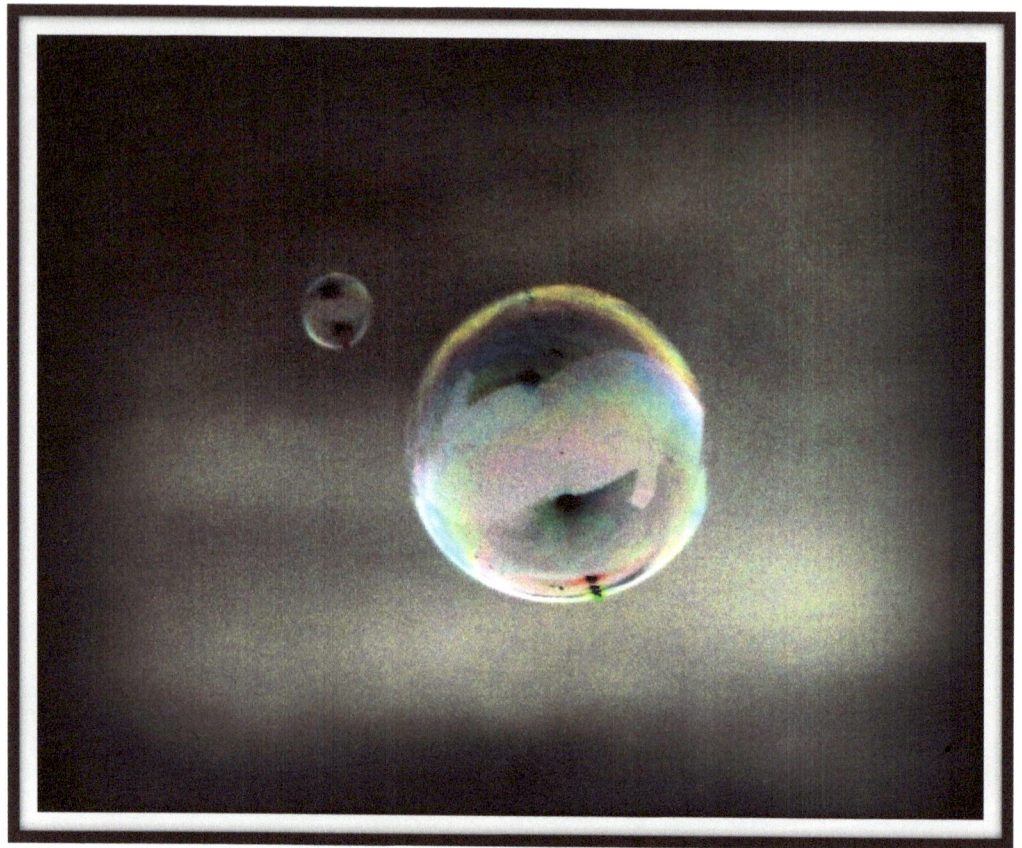

South Sea Bubble?

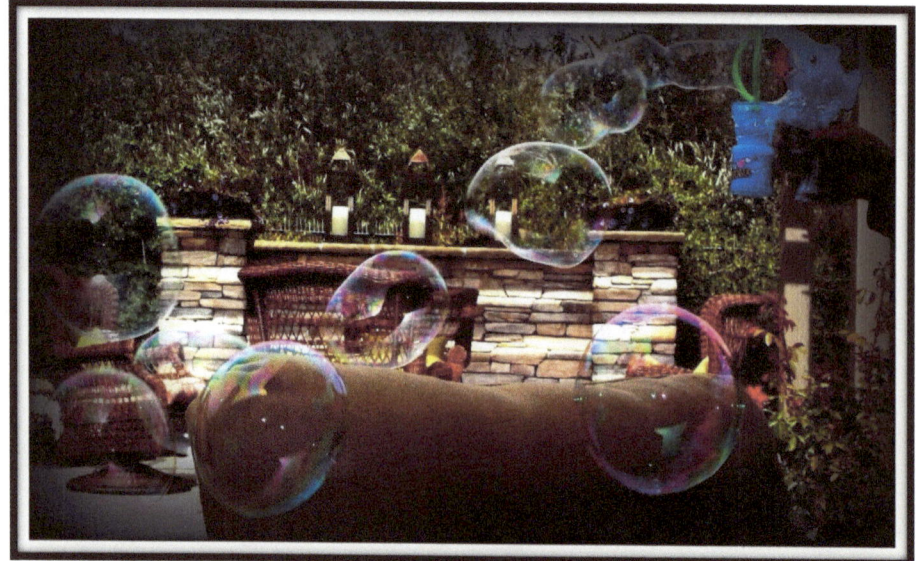

Trevor's Bubbles

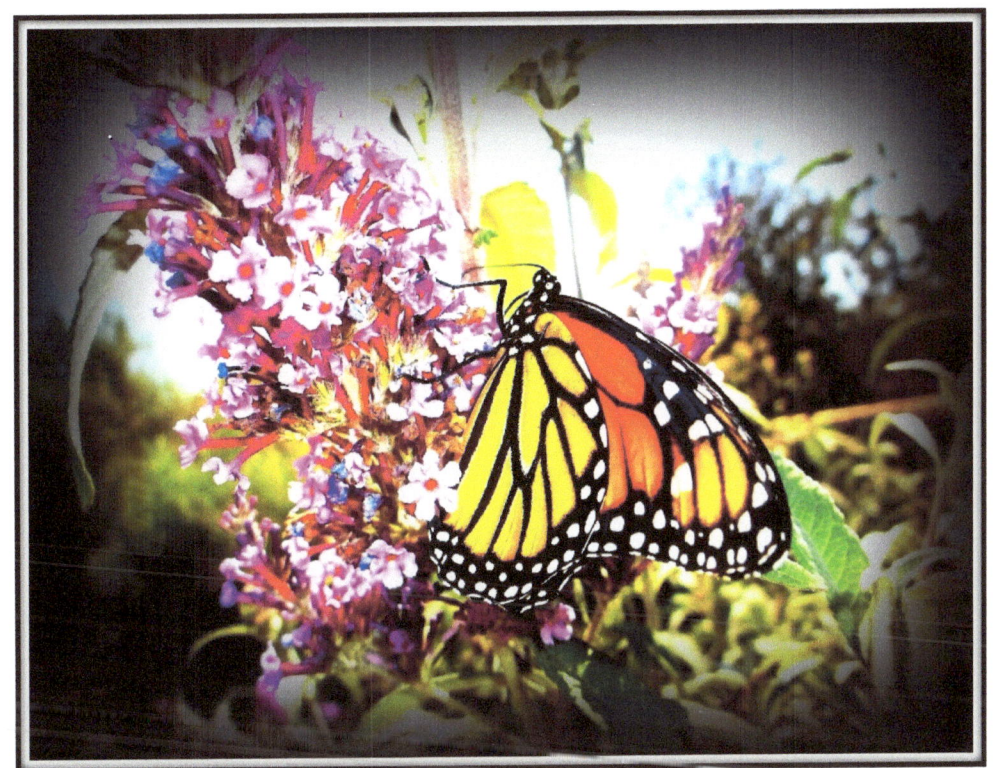

Come Fly with Me

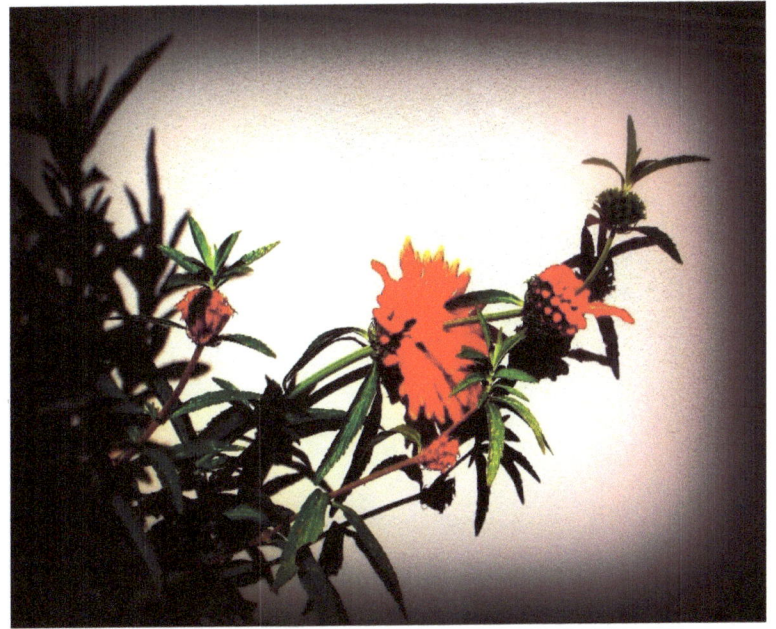

Careful, It Could be a Plant

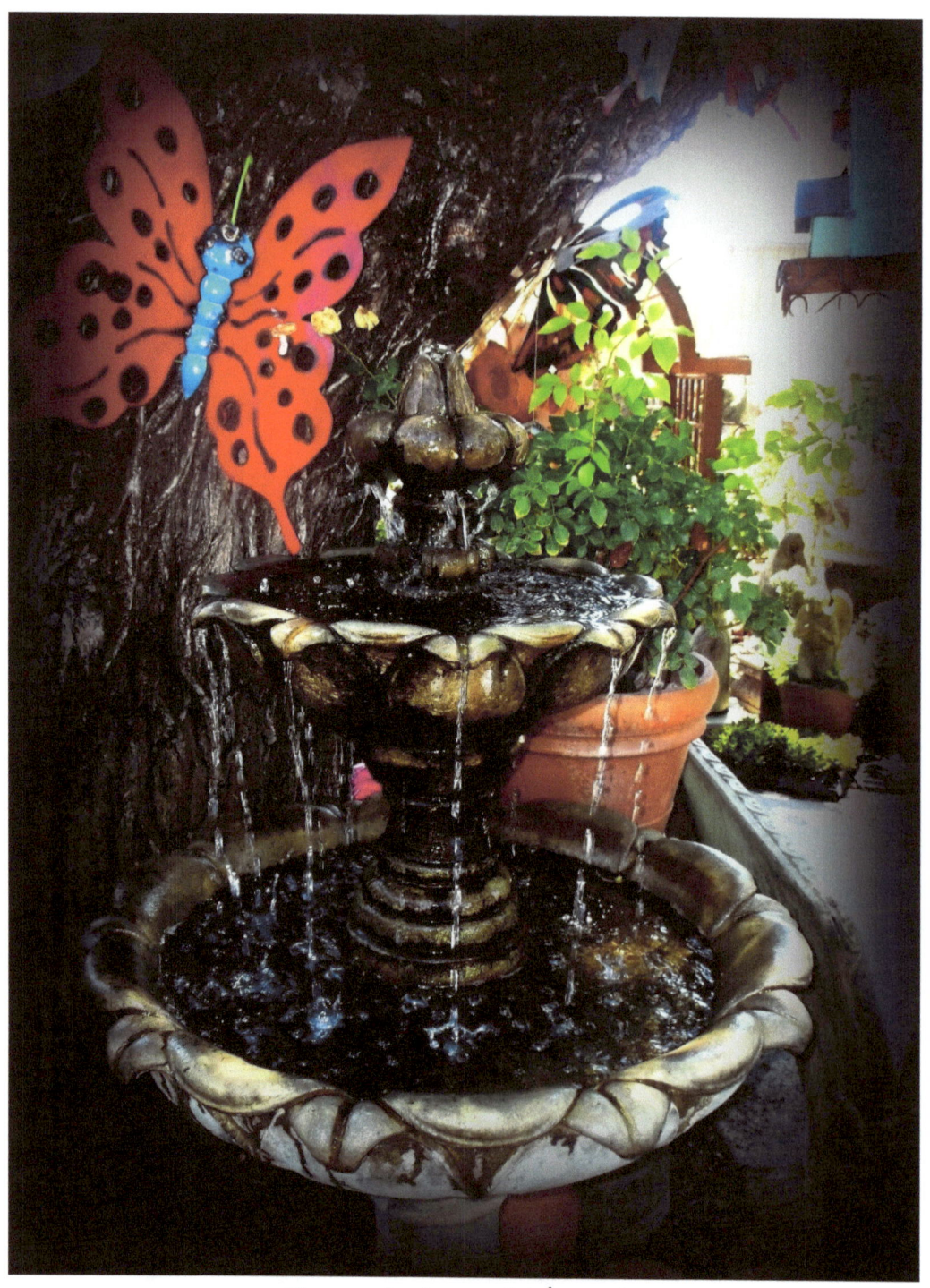

Fountain of Youth

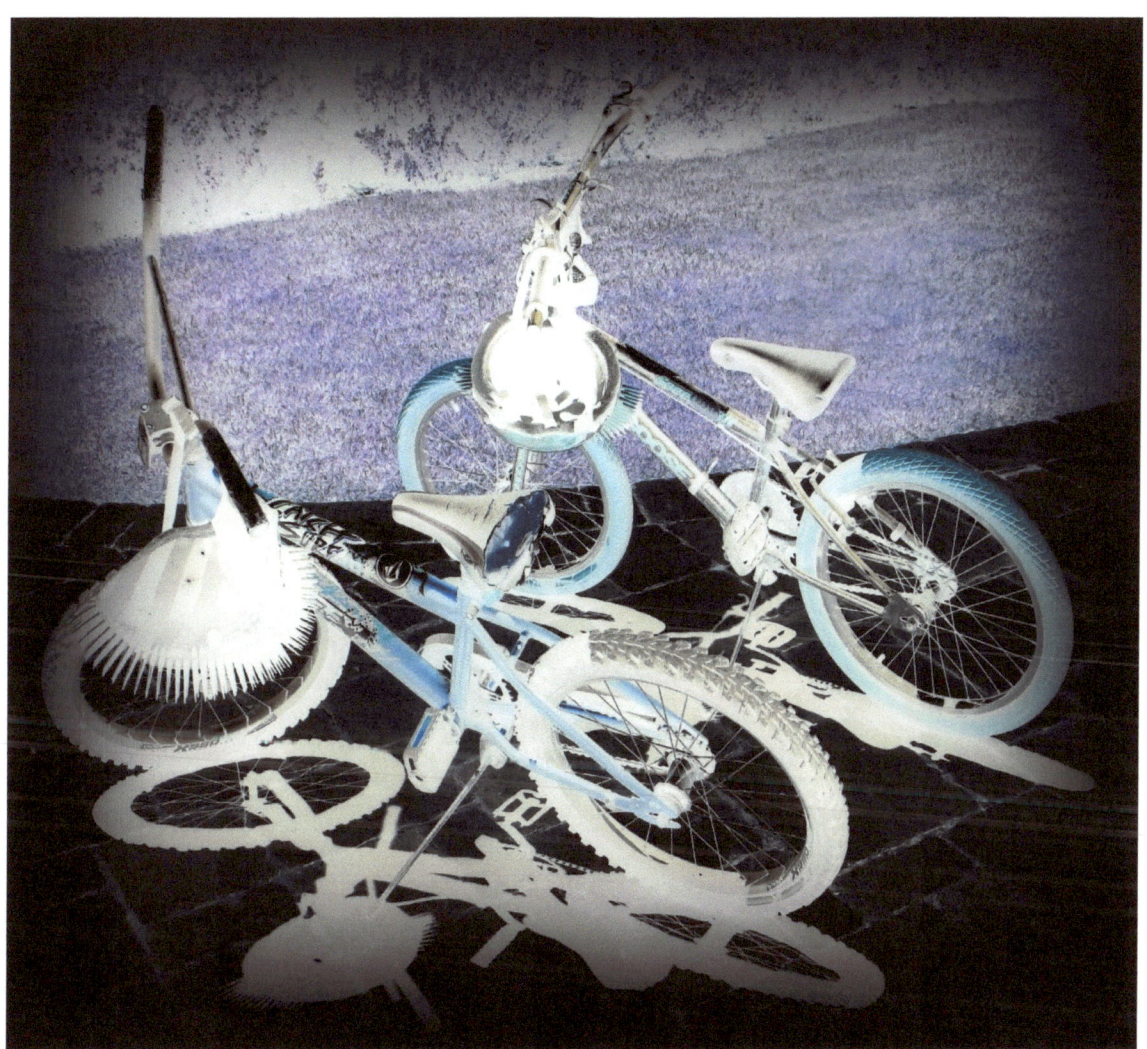

California Bikes

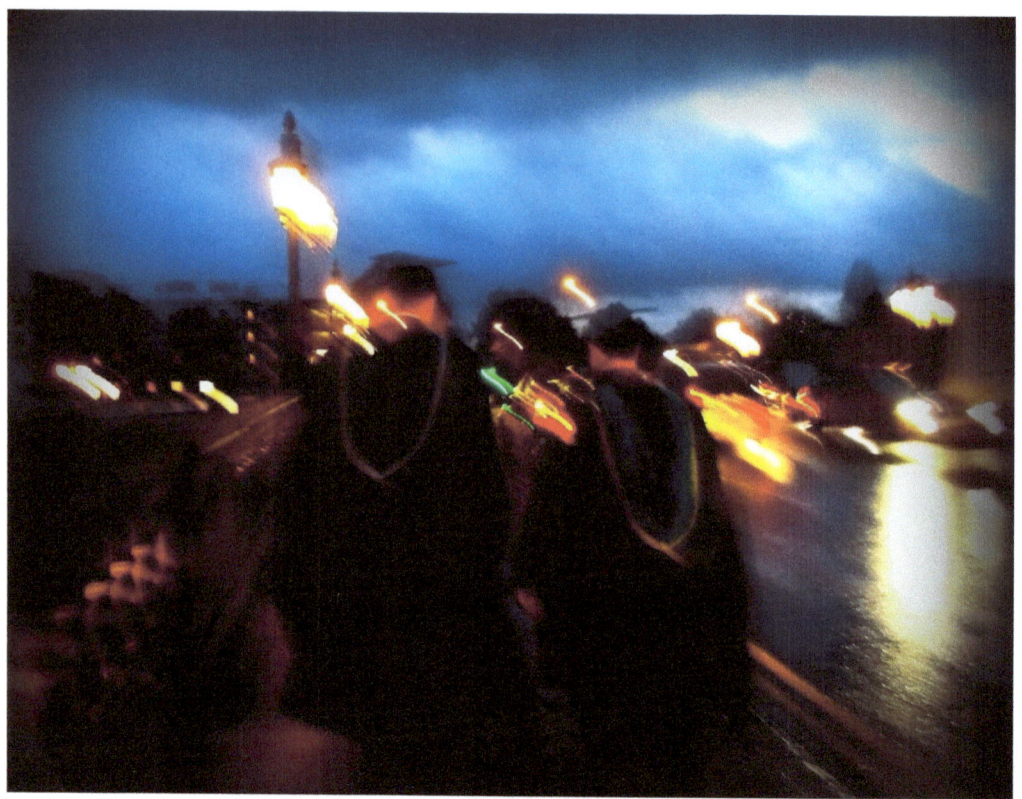

Graduation – University of Worcester

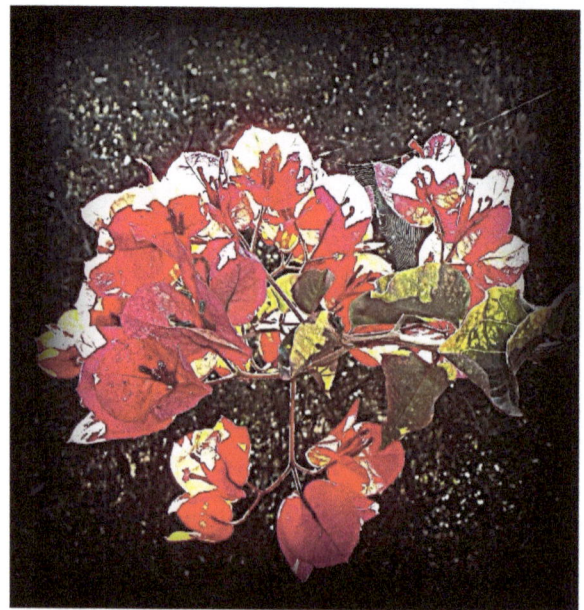

Bloomin' LA

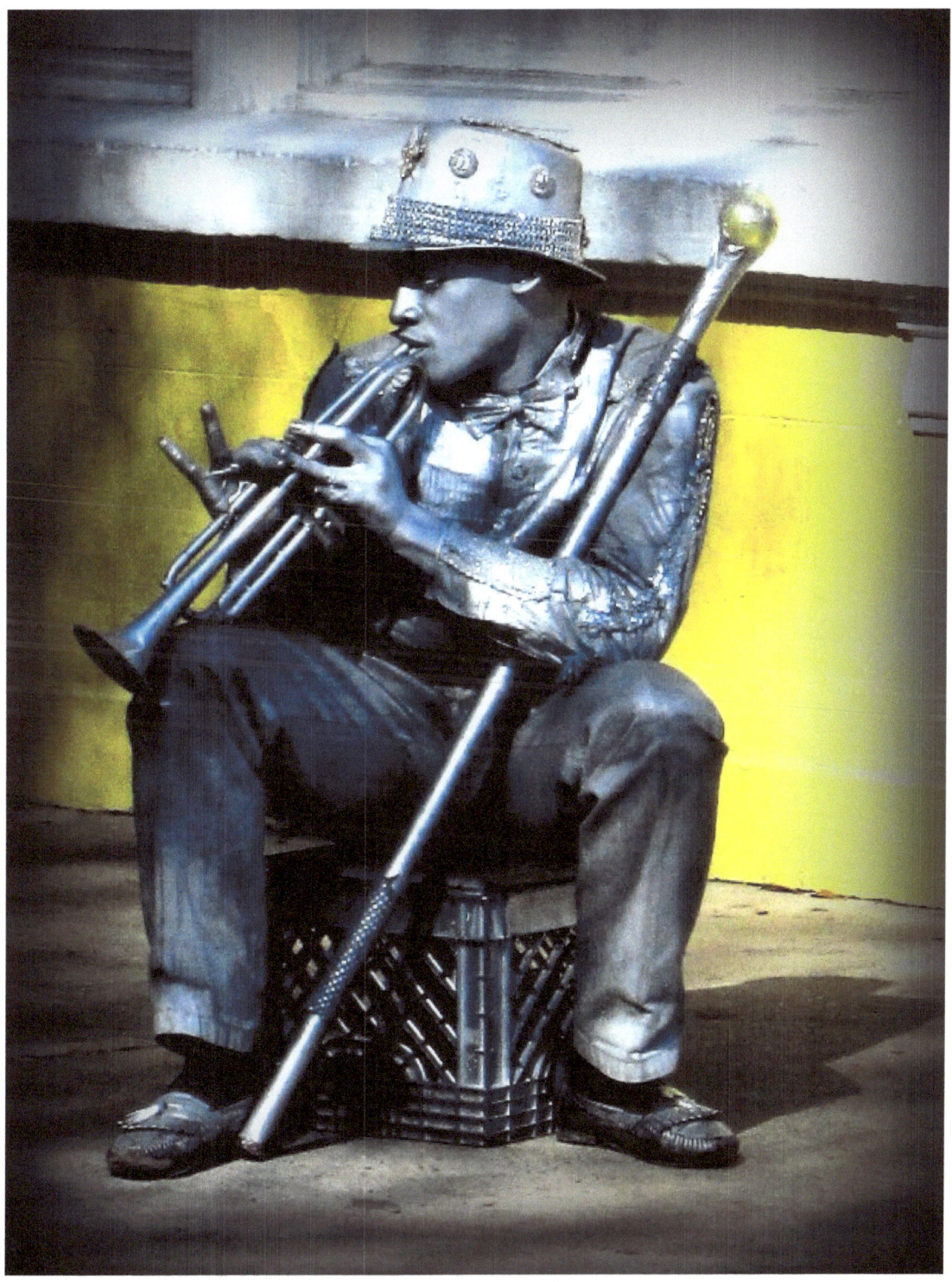

Street Performer – New Orleans

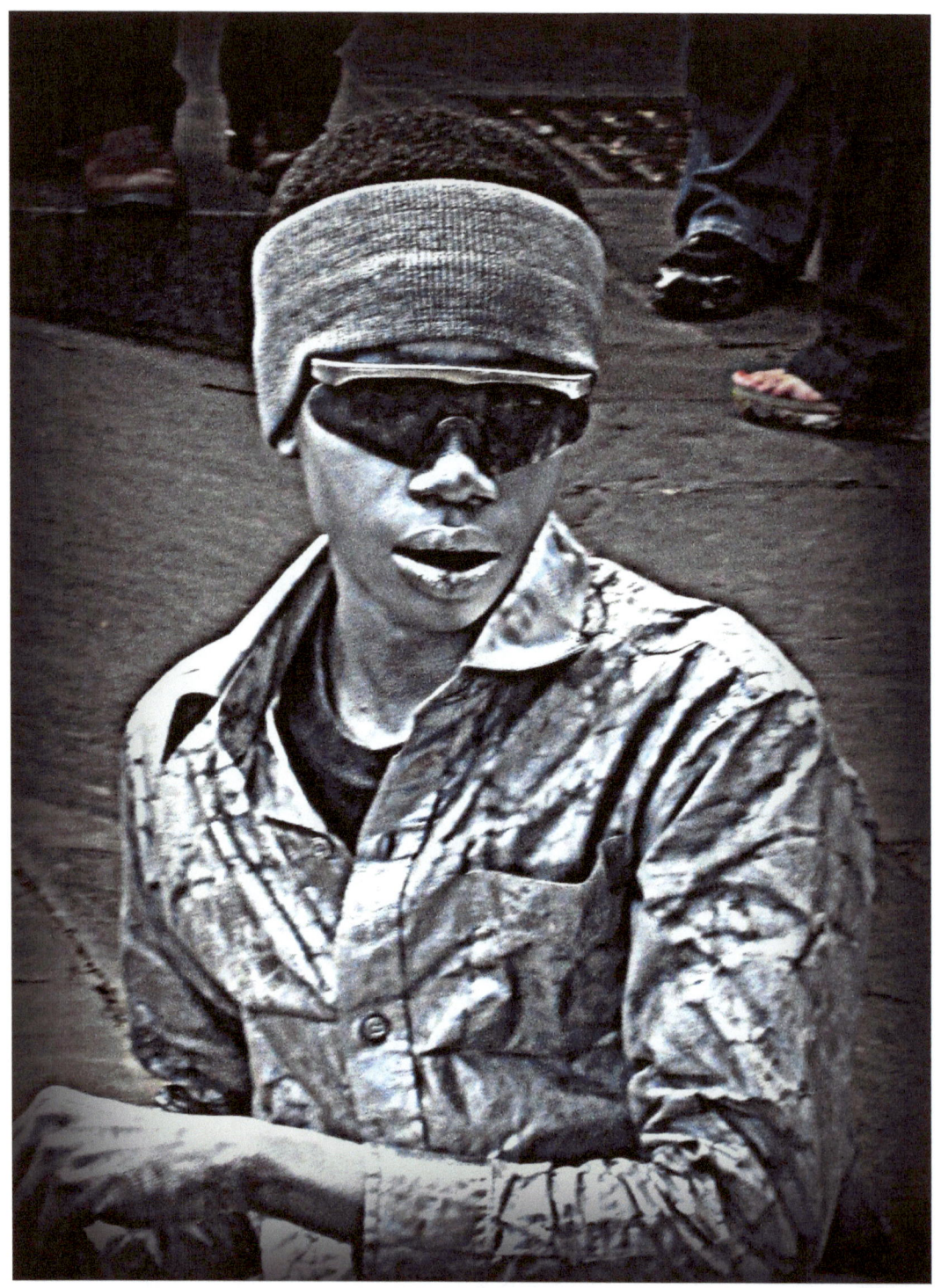

Long John Silver – New Orleans

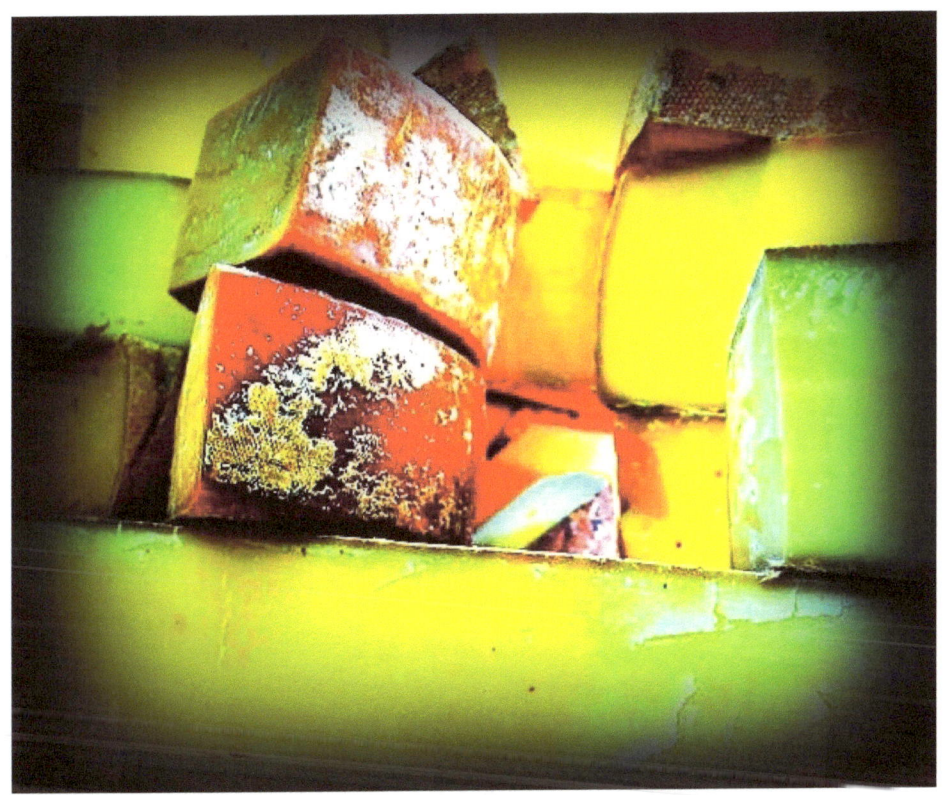

Cheese

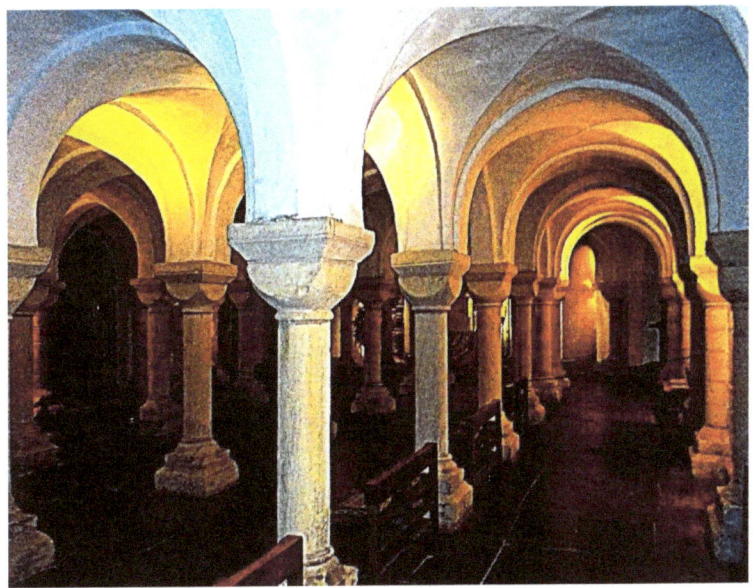

Tales from the Crypt

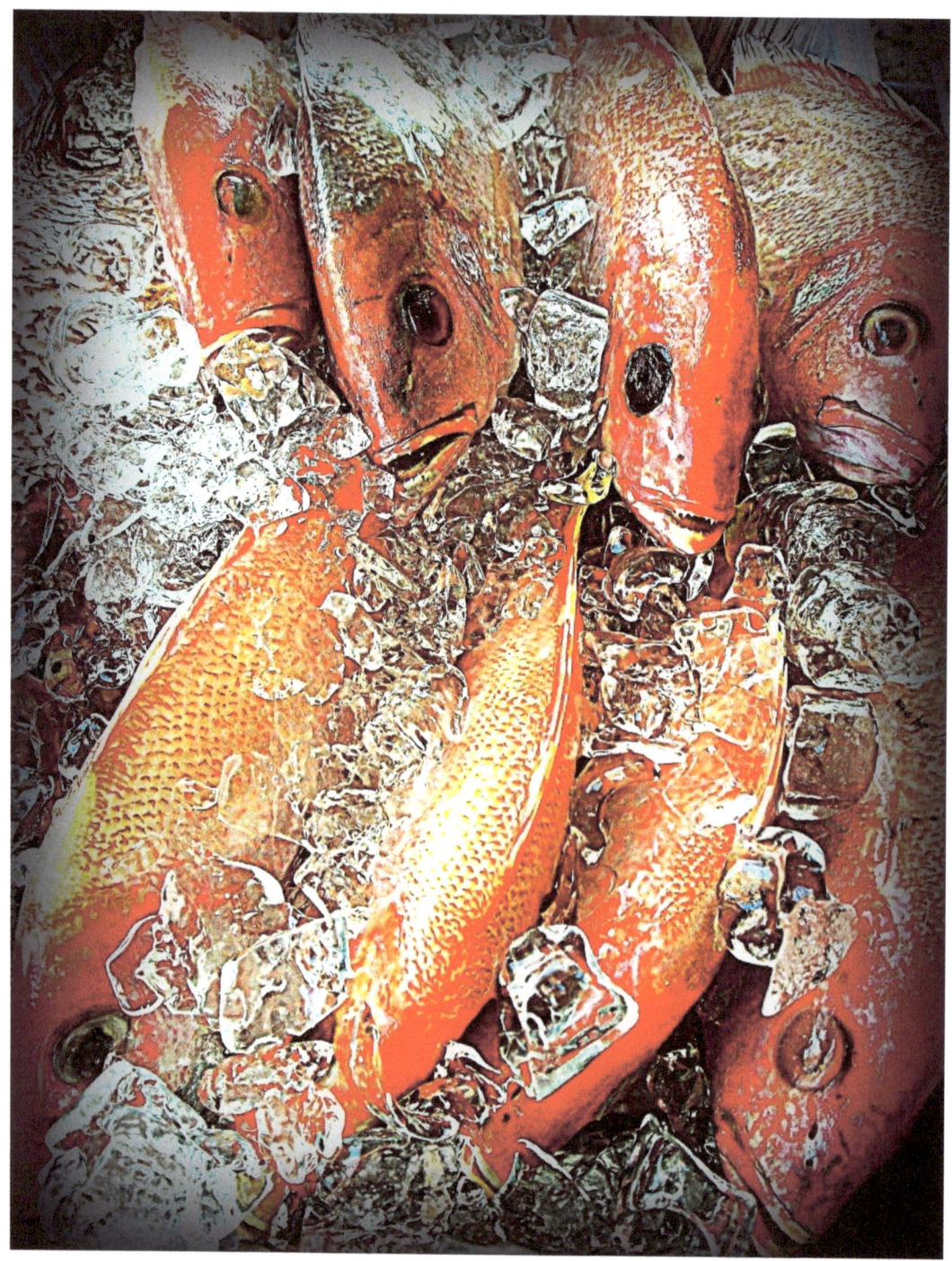

Snapper Snap

www.ingramcontent.com/pod-product-compliance
Lightning Source LLC
Chambersburg PA
CBHW051100180526
45172CB00002B/718